Welsh Sail

Welsh Sail

A pictorial history by Susan Campbell-Jones

with a foreword by Alun Richards

Gomer Press

For my children
GUY, LYN and VICKI

Contents

First printed 1976

© Gomer Press/S. Campbell-Jones

Published by
Gomer Press

Printed by
J D Lewis & Sons Ltd
Gomer Press
Llandysul
Dyfed
Wales

Designed by
Roger Lloyd Jones

SBN 85088 353 9

Acknowledgements

I am very grateful to those institutions and individuals listed below who supplied me with photographs and answered my questions patiently and helpfully. I am particularly indebted to Mrs. G. M. Davies who drew the line illustrations to the introduction, and to the late Mr. E. Beynon Davies, the late Captain Danny Evans, Miss Dora Evans, Mr. Jack James, Capt. T. G. James, the late Captain Otway Jones, and Mr. Roderick Cheley for providing me with much useful information.

SOURCES FOR THE ILLUSTRATIONS

Newport Public Library: 2, 47; National Library of Wales: 3, 8, 11, 12, 18, 19, 43, 51; Glamorgan Record Office: 4, 5, 7, 52; National Museum of Wales: 6, 24, 33, 50, 52, 55, 61, 63; Royal Institution of South Wales: 9, 48, 74; Llanelli Public Library: 10; Cardiff Public Library: 13; National Maritime Museum: 14, 15, 16, 57, 68a, 75; Cardiganshire Joint Library: 25, 26; Merioneth Record Office: 28, 30, 31, 35; Caernarvon Record Office: 34, 36, 37, 53; Flint Record Office: 40, 41, 42, 44, 45, 46, 56; Victoria & Albert Museum: 49; Ceredigion Museum: 66; Lancaster City Museum: 70. Author's Collection: Frontispiece, 20, 27, 67, 68, 69, 72, 77; Roger Worsley: 17; Alun Jones, 21; Gareth Mills, 29, 64; T. Stephenson & Sons, Ltd., 52, 59; Frank Bell: 38; Douglas Hague: 39, 54; Captain Frank Parker: 58; the late Capt. Danny Evans: 60, 62; David Lewis Jones & the Cardiganshire Antiquarian Society: 65; R. W. Cheley: 71; Captain Hoskin Evans: 73; Mr. & Mrs. Williams: 76.

List of Illustrations

Foreword

Years ago, I had the luck to meet a man who at fourteen had sailed out of Cardiff on the sister ship of the *Cutty Sark,* in passage to Iquique in South America, and upon his lips were the phrases of the sea, 'Falmouth for orders, Odessa for grain', and frequent scornful references to 'featherbed bosuns' and the 'soft' conditions which have prevailed aboard ship since. He had slept on donkey's breakfasts, tapped out weevils from salt tack biscuits, seen his Roath Park schoolmate shot in the back by a Spanish sentry, and ended up older and wiser with three golden guineas in his belt, having been, in the words of blue water men, 'all over'.

Nothing makes more impression on the mind than the whiff of reality which sometimes accompanies the reminiscences of such old men for they retain the prejudices of the past, the telling attitudes which often escape the historian, and upon picking up this book, I could not help but imagine his delight, had he the luck to hold it in his hands. How he would have thumbed the photographs, and in my mind's eye, I can see him turning them this way and that in order to study the standing rigging, the names of some of these handsome ships no doubt familiar to him, and perhaps even those of their masters. Perhaps he could have told me that the Portmadoc ship, *Pride of Wales*, survived two tornadoes in the Caribbean, that it was the skipper's daughter, Jenny, whose likeness was carved on the figurehead in India, or that Captain Dai Williams of St. Dogmaels, master of the four masted barque *Bellands,* kept the best fed apprentices on the Cape Horn run. If he could not, then he would know when he had read on, and I can picture his gnarled face creasing with pleasure at the abundance of detail within.

For us, too, nothing has ever quite taken the place of the sailing ship, certainly not in looks, and however well-proportioned a modern vessel may be, it is doubtful if such an intimate personal relationship between a mechanically driven vessel and her officers and crew, ever existed in the same way as the rapport between a sailing vessel and her men, which perhaps explains the descriptions of seamen of their favourite vessels. 'A regular roll-along, blow-along old girl' she might be, or one to be 'driven hard and never humoured'. The personality of ships was thus discussed, no doubt in the same detail as a particular master, and although the lives of ships were all too often documented in a meagre way, each one had her own story, her own idiosyncracies, and this book, in addition to an excellently illustrated account of vessels originating around our coast of Wales, also deals with some of the stories behind the facts.

And what stories they were! Here is the mystery of the barque *Usk* returned fully laden to Newport with her hatches unopened, her master, Captain Digby Mathias being summarily convinced after a visit from the Almighty that to proceed further around Cape Horn would result in disaster. You might imagine that he was dismissed, but no one knows what he felt when some months later the vessel proceeded under a new master and came to the exact end predicted in precisely the same latitudes.

Such stories abound in the lore of the sea, and while much must be left to speculation, a good deal is known about the men who sailed and built the ships, and Welsh seamen had an honoured name in the great ports of the world. Conrad himself, in a reminiscence of one of his old captains states that he had served his time in the copper ore trade between Swansea and the Chilean coast, 'coal out and ore in, deep-loaded both ways, as if in wanton defiance of the great Cape Horn seas, a work this for staunch ships . . . a whole fleet of copper-bottomed barques, as strong in rib and planking, as well found in gear as ever was sent upon the seas, manned by hardy crews and young masters'.

"That was the school I was trained in," the Captain told Conrad, "almost boastfully," and to have been bred in the copper ore trade was a mark of distinction. At times, we are told, the strain of carrying these heavy cargoes around the Horn was so great that on many occasions, it was a case of pump or sink, and there is an eye-witness account of an old Swansea barque afloat just after the first war. 'The pumps on board bore silent testimony to their own importance, for their fly wheel handles extended right across the main deck from pin rail to pin rail and the bushes of the bearings were so worn as to hint at long and continuous spells of pumping when every sea poured across the main deck, waist high'.

The dangers have never ceased. Leaks, lee shores, the King's enemies, and pirates were said to be the principal hazards which faced seamen up to the end of the Nineteenth Century, but the greatest drain on manhood was probably due to disease, and this due to ignorance, foul water and overcrowded focsles. The ignorance is most amusingly revealed in the yarn of the ship's captain who, despairing of the number of medicants rolling loose in his locker, divided them willy nilly into two drawers, labelling them Above and Below so that seamen reporting sick were required to state the position of the ailment before qualifying for a remedy. But for many there was no remedy and no hope, as the records show. There was once a cemetery in Cuba known as the Swansea Cemetery because of the number of Swansea seamen who had died there of yellow fever, and we can gather the toll of this disease from a register of dead men's effects kept in the port in the year 1862. Of the vessels arriving in that year, 'the *San Jose* lost two of her crew from yellow fever at Cuba, the *Florence*—one, the *Cornwall* lost ten of her crew from the same disease, five at Cuba and five at sea; the *Ellen* lost eight, seven at Havannah, and one on the passage home; the *Hampshire*—one; *Mangosteen*—one; the *Countess of Bective* lost five of her men from yellow fever and one of brain fever; the *Dorsetshire* and *Cobrero* each lost four from yellow fever at Cuba'.

The only outbreak of this disease ever to occur in the British Isles was brought to Swansea by the barque *Hecla* who first showed her light off Mumbles Head at 9 pm on September 8th 1865. Within three weeks, fifteen people had died. At first, the master had attempted to conceal the presence of disease and the Board of Customs concluded that 'there had been a great irregularity and neglect on the part of all persons on board'. Such was the fear of disease in general that as late as 1922, there is a case minuted in the Swansea Harbour Trust's records of the Committee declining to censure a pilot for refusing to go aboard the *S.S. British Isles* which arrived with a case of smallpox on board.

Wales too, had her share of pirates and the reader will learn that at one time, Cardiff was so notorious a haunt of pirates that the City's merchants dared not admit they were from there when abroad, and many a promontory along the Welsh coast once displayed gallows where convicted freebooters were left 'a sun-drying like a scarecrow', their whitening bones dangling as a warning to others who might be tempted to stray from the straight and narrow. Pembrokeshire's Captain Bartholomew Roberts— 'the worshipful Mr. Roberts'—'better a pirate and a commander be, than a common man'—laid down a special clause in his code of articles stating that his musicians 'were to have rest on the Sabbath day, but on the other six days and nights, none without special favour!' When his crew became unruly, 'he put on a rough deportment and a more magisterial presence toward them, correcting where he saw fit, and if any seemed to resent his useage, he told them, they might go ashore and take satisfaction of him if they thought fit, at sword or pistol, for he neither valued nor feared any of them!'

But it is with the record of merchant shipping, the builders, the traders, and those who had to do with the lawful commerce of the sea that this book concerns itself in the main. Each port and harbour in Wales is dealt with and much of the information will remain in the mind long after the book is closed. Anyone, for example, who has ever asked himself the reason for the extraordinary number of master mariners who hailed from Cardiganshire will find part of the answer in the account of the schoolmistress, Sarah Jane Rees of Llangrannog who taught navigation in the village school, having qualified herself for the certificate of master mariner.

In short, this book is a delight to all who love the sea, but perhaps it is the ships themselves, long gone now, which stand out so poignantly from these pages and cause the most questions to be asked. When David

Jones's *Blodwen,* Portmadoc built and manned, made the record run from Indian Tickle, Labrador, to Patras, Greece, in twenty-two days, what excitement there must have been. For on that golden day, she was not merely the equal in speed and looks of anything carrying sail on the western ocean, but top dog! One can imagine their pride, and it only remains for me to say that a good measure of that pride can rightfully be felt by the author of this book in whose debt all its readers will remain.

ALUN RICHARDS

Chapter 1
An Historical Note

Ships with sails have been a familiar sight off the coasts of Wales since prehistoric times, and 'the grey waters of the Irish Sea as bright with Neolithic argonauts as the Western Pacific is today'. These narrow seas were criss-crossed with sea-lanes traversed by craft sailing to and from Spain and France. The builders of the great megalithic monuments found along its coasts, brought their culture from the Iberian peninsula, through France, across Cornwall to Pembrokeshire, using the trans-peninsular route popular with these early seamen who disliked sailing around stormy headlands. Bronze Age merchants regularly used these routes to Ireland. The earliest 'ship' known in Wales is the small Bronze Age ceremonial oak bowl (now in the National Museum of Wales), inlaid with gold and carved to represent a ship, dug up at Caergwrle in Flintshire last century, near a hill-fort which commanded a good view of the Dee estuary. Among the earliest sea-going craft were the great wooden rafts, each with a single leather sail, which were probably used to transport the blue stones from the Preseli Mountains along the Cleddau estuary to the Severn Sea and so to the mouth of the Avon and Stonehenge. Then came the curraghs or coracles of wickerwork covered with hides—described by Pliny. These could be large enough to carry twenty men and support a mast, and when Julius Caesar arrived in Gaul, he found not only the curraghs in use along the whole Atlantic seaboard, but also large carvel-built

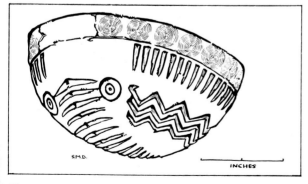

Fig. 1

Fig. 2

flat-bottomed ships with high poops and sterns and leather sails, which rode the sea well and were surprisingly manoeuvrable.

The Romans developed ports along this seaboard, for example at Cardiff and Caernarvon. The Celtic saints regularly used the prehistoric seaways in the early Middle Ages for their many crusading journeys. But their curraghs were followed closely by the longships of the Vikings who repeatedly sacked the lonely monastic settlements the saints had founded along these coasts: their painted sails and the awesomely-carved dragon heads of their ships became a dreaded sight. They wintered frequently in *Mid Fjödr Havn* (Milford Haven), whose winding fiords must have reminded them pleasantly of home. A Viking ship dating from A.D. 900 was found when the Alexandra Dock was being constructed at Newport, Monmouthshire in 1878, and proved to be a clinker-built boat of Danzig oak, seventy feet long by seventeen to twenty feet broad. When eventually the Vikings ceased their raids and settled on the shores they had so long plundered, with their superb ships and expert knowledge of the sea, they took the lead in the sea-trade of the Middle Ages, according to that mine of information about twelfth-century Wales, *Giraldus Cambrensis*. The ships used were still of the Viking type which are so beautifully and clearly depicted on the Bayeux Tapestry, but were more capacious and a great deal slower than their prototypes. Some small seaports owed their prosperity at this time to the pilgrim traffic which was

Fig. 3

considerable—especially after the Pope decreed that two pilgrimages to St. Davids were the equivalent of one to Rome. Their ships were generally built of locally-grown timber: in Swansea, charters survive which show the rights of the burgesses of the twelfth and fourteenth centuries to cut oak timber for building and repairing boats: a tax of one shilling was paid on each vessel built. We know few details of their construction but accounts survive for work on the King's barge at Carmarthen in 1428: wages were sixpence a day for the head carpenter and threepence a day for the labourers. Vessels were frequently described as 'Cogs'—that is a small broadly-built cargo ship: the *Coga Sanctie Marie* of Conway, *Seynt Marie Cogge* of Pembroke, *Cogge John* of Kidwelly.

While most mediaeval ships had been built like galleys with a single short mast and sail, by the

sixteenth century the three-masted sailing ship had been developed with at least half a dozen sails.

The Port Books which originated with the measures taken to improve the administration of the English Customs revenue and to establish effective control over the coasting trade of the realm towards the middle of the 1500s, kept careful records of the foreign trade in these waters, hitherto dominantly an inward traffic connected with the salt and wine trades and mainly carried on by the sailors and shipping drawn from Brittany. But during Elizabeth's reign the Port books reveal considerable activity on the part of both native merchants and shipping. Exports increased in the 1600s owing to the development of the slate industry and the mineral resources of Wales and the North-West, notably coal, iron and to some extent, lead and copper. Irish timber was imported in increasing amounts, pointing to a more active shipbuilding industry, which reflected the general encouragement given to national commerce at this time. Shipmen became more adventurous, Welsh sailors joined eagerly in the quest for the New World: several sailed with Sir Francis Drake and Sir Humphrey Gilbert, including Sir Miles Morgan of Tredegar who commanded the *Red Lyon* of 110 tons,

Fig. 5

in the little fleet which Gilbert led in 1578, to plant an English colony in North America.

The most developed region economically was South Wales, from Chepstow to Milford which possessed the greatest number of ships then owned in Wales. In the

Fig. 4

north, Beaumaris, Caernarvon, Conway and Chester were prosperous seaport towns but Cardigan Bay possessed only little fishing boats used in the herring trade. The size of the ships varied from six to eighty tons but the average size was around twenty to thirty tons. Ships of forty tons or over—the 'topmen', were few and there were more in Glamorganshire and Monmouthshire than in all the other parts of Wales put together, in the 1500s. For all their small size, a large number of men were employed in the vessels—ten or twelve or sixteen on the ships of forty or fifty tons, and four or five even on the little ships of six to ten tons. By the 1700s the technical advances in rigging were so great that the vessels were more easily handled and two or three were sufficient, and in the golden age of merchant shipping in the 1800s, the much larger vessels carried no more crew than had the little ships of earlier days.

Piracy was always a problem for the many little concealed creeks provided safe havens and covers for their nefarious purposes, and not until the reign of Elizabeth were really effective efforts made to protect legitimate trade from freebooters. It was considered adviseable for vessels to sail in convoys for protection. Brittany was one of the principal haunts—Lundy another: at the beginning of the fifteenth century a Breton pirate named Colyn Dolphin terrorized shipping in the Severn Sea—he took Sir Harry Stradling of St. Donat's prisoner off the Glamorgan coast, for a ransom of £1,400. But much of the central government's work was nullified because the pirates freely bribed sheriffs, justices and customs officers.

The Queen's Remembrancer Roll, 1562, states of Caldy Island: 'Here the pirates are wount many tymes to victual theymselves of sheepe and other provisions sometyme without leave of the owners. Milford is ye grete resort and socoure of all piratts.' In the 1500s Cardiff was so notorious as a haunt of pirates that Cardiff merchants abroad dared not admit that they hailed from there. Caldy Island was used by a sea-raider of another kind during the War for American Independence: John Paul Jones frequently watered his privateer *The Ranger* there.

The 1700s were the heyday of the smuggling trade. The cost of the wars with France was very high and to defray them the Government placed heavy duties on a large number of articles—tea, tobacco and liqueurs, salt, soap, candles and oil among them. One famous smuggler Thomas Knight had his headquarters on Barry Island, a brig with twenty-four guns and a crew of forty. A great deal of smuggling went on in Cardigan Bay too. The captain of the revenue cutter *Hector* (together with the *Lord North* and the *Cardigan*) spent much time trying to capture the armed cruiser named *Fox* which was engaged in smuggling between the Bristol channel and Anglesey. She was a vessel of 100 tons and forty-five crew.

Fig. 6

The 1800s ushered in the great age of sail, when expanding markets overseas and increased capital circulating, acted as a spur to commercial and industrial expansion and shipbuilding: an outstanding example is that of William Madocks and the 'Wonder of Wales'—his reclamation of Traethmawr to make Portmadoc—opened in 1824 to become **the** port for the export of Ffestiniog slates, at a cost of £160,000. At the other end of Cardigan Bay eleven years later, tiny New Quay found it worthwhile to float a harbour company to build a stone pier for £7,000 and led the way in shipbuilding with around 250 ships being built or owned here. The ports were crowded with native-built ships, barques, brigs, brigantines, barquentines, schooners, ketches, snows, smacks and sloops.

Steamships brought to an end the boom in sail—
steam packet companies had penetrated these waters
as early as 1819, and later further competition was
provided by the railways and finally by the motor lorry
which was able to carry goods to the little towns once
reachable only by sea.

Today in a few ports on this coast, vast acres of docks
crammed with shipping, bear witness to a long and
profitable career for shipowners and merchants:
elsewhere only the ruins of a quay, an overgrown
limekiln, rusting chains and rotting bollards bear
witness to a once active commercial life, forgotten
men and vanished ships.

In selecting the many illustrations for this book, I
have tried to bring the past to life in a region which is
usually passed over by writers of maritime history
although not indeed by local historians to whose
patient work I owe a great deal. It was a region with a
long tradition of sea-faring and has contributed much
towards Britain's commercial prosperity. Today this
area still exerts a fascination for the small-boat sailor
who makes our often grey Western waters truly bright
with the multi-coloured sails and hulls of innumerable
small craft. But the merchant sailor has gone forever,
though something of his courage and expertise and
love for the sea-life—hard though it was in sailing
ships—is still to be found there.

Chapter 2
Around the Ports

For Newport, a new port in the 1300s, with an established foreign trade since Elizabethan times, the opening of the Monmouthshire Canal in 1796, began an era of prosperity which made this town on the River Usk, at its mouth the deepest river in the British Isles, one of the chief coal ports in Britain. The Town Dock was opened in 1842 and the Alexandra Dock in 1875. The wooden barque with the rail around her poop and stern decoration characteristic of Scandinavian vessels is the *Maria Margretta Timra* built in Sweden in 1877, unloading timber in the Alexandra Dock in 1905. One of the stern hold ports through which long balks of timber could be conveniently loaded, can clearly be seen. Some have already been cleared and are being fastened into a raft by one man watched with absorbed interest by a small boy. To her left is another timber barque, her decks piled with long poles and her sides painted with gunports, a form of decoration established in the early 1800s, which remained popular for over a century. The presence of several very large sailing vessels in the Docks is typical of that era—when the smaller barques and schooners were restricted to some coasting trades and only the enormous four-masted barques, designed primarily as carriers rather than clippers, although they were often capable of smart passages, could compete economically with steamships.

2   Alexandra Dock, Newport

A good crowd has gathered to see an unidentified topsail schooner leaving the Bute Dock in 1907; the Dock Offices are on the right. Cardiff's first Dock was built by the second Marquess of Bute, a man of foresight and energy, in 1839. In the early days of coal-exporting from Cardiff the cargoes were mostly carried in vessels from other ports: shipowning in Cardiff did not become significant until the era of large steamships, although small shipyards had existed there since 1813 when Joseph Davies leased the old Town Quay and built a half-tide dock on the River Taff between the Theatre and the old Western Mail buildings. Between 1829 and 1850 Richard Tredwen had a shipyard at the head of the West Bute Dock, adjoining the site of the later Mount Stuart Ship-repairing Works.

The West Bute Dock was designed to accommodate small vessels only and in 1855 the Bute East Dock was completed by the fourth Marquess, to harbour larger vessels. In 1875 the Roath Basin was opened but in the next five years traffic in the Bute Docks increased by 73% which taxed their capacity to its maximum: delays and congestion continued and frequent collisions took place between waiting vessels anchored in Cardiff Roads.

3   Dock Offices at Cardiff (The *Sphere* 1907)

Consequently a group of dissatisfied coal owners developed the Penarth Docks on the Ely River, photographed below in 1883 with innumerable square-riggers queueing to load coal. At high tide Penarth Dock was virtually a tidal harbour and a quicker dispatch was possible than from the Bute Docks.

4   Penarth Dock, May 1883

The pressure on Cardiff was also relieved by the development of Barry Docks by the former topsawyer and leading coalowner David Davies of Llandinam. In 1880 Barry was a hamlet of seventeen houses; nine years later David Davies had created the largest coal exporting docks in the world. Below the four-masted barque, *Chamber of Commerce,* loaded with coal for the West Coast of South America is leaving Barry, the pilot is aboard and she has his cutter in tow.

5   Entrance to Barry Dock

The barque *Terra Nova*, fitted with an auxiliary engine is seen leaving Cardiff in 1910 with Captain Robert Falcon Scott on board, bound for his fatal Antarctic expedition. Appropriately she is escorted by the Cardiff tug *Falcon*. Penarth Head is in the background. Captain Scott wrote subsequently in his journal as the vessel forged her way south through the pack ice:

The ship behaved splendidly—no other ship not even the *Discovery* would have come through so well. As a result I have grown strongly attached to the *Terra Nova*. As she bumped the floes with mighty shocks, crushing and grinding her way through some with her ironshod bow, twisting and turning to avoid others, she seemed like a living thing, fighting a great fight.

6   *Terra Nova* leaving Cardiff 1910

The steel ship *Verajean* launched in 1891 by
A. McMillan, Dunbarton, who built many well-known
iron and steel ships and barques. While bound for
Peru with patent fuel from Cardiff, in August 1908, a
full gale blew up and in very heavy seas she was driven
ashore at Rhoose Point near Barry.

7   *S.S. Verajean* wrecked off Rhoose Point

The building of these new docks and harbours created a huge demand for limestone from the little port of Aberthaw—coasters like the *Fonmon Castle,* the *Ferrett* and the *Providence* sailed regularly from the mouth of the Thaw to Newport, Cardiff, Barry, Porthcawl, Aberavon, Port Talbot, Neath and Swansea. But the trade virtually ceased in 1900 and the site of the old port is now overshadowed by a huge Power Station. The tidal creek of Porthcawl, converted into a harbour in 1830 was also once thronged with shipping, but its coal trade was drawn away by Barry Dock and subsequently by Port Talbot whose docks were expanded in 1898, and Porthcawl became a holiday resort.

Below is a panorama of Swansea Harbour and docks from Kilvey Hill, taken in 1881 to commemorate the opening of the massive Prince of Wales Dock on the left. Although the copper ore trade on which her prosperity was founded was then declining, Swansea's exports of coal, patent fuel and anthracite more than justified the expansion.

8   The Swansea Harbour and Docks

The copper-ore barque *Zeta* in Swansea's North Docks. She was the first sailing vessel in Swansea to be fitted with a steam auxiliary, and was built at Glasgow in 1865 by Alexander Stephen. She was one of the many small, but efficient and sturdy, barques built to carry ore from Chile to Britain's leading copper-smelting port. The *Zeta* was part of the fleet of Henry Bath, most of whose vessels were named after the letters of the Greek alphabet. Swansea copper-ore barques were noted for their smart performances and some of the fastest passages to South America were made in Swansea-owned vessels:

Bath's *Kappa* sailed from Swansea to Valparaiso in seventy-one days, but the unbroken record was held by the *Pacific* owned by Richards, Power & Company of Swansea: Barrow—Valparaiso in sixty-eight days. The 750 ton iron barque *Aberlemno* was probably the last sailing ship to carry a copper cargo to Swansea, arriving back in the port in 1902.

The dangerous little limestone coves of the Gower coast are no longer visited by North Devon vessels, for the once flourishing trade ended about 1900—lime having been replaced by artificial fertilisers. Little

9   The *Zeta* at Swansea

remains to show that places such as Port Eynon, Llanmorlais, Llanmadoc and Penclawdd were once busy little ports. At Penclawdd the chief export was coal, not limestone, shipped to Devon, Cornwall and Ireland, and copper ore was imported from Cornwall and Anglesey for Benson's Copper Works. To the north of the Railway Inn it is still possible to detect the remains of the harbour built in 1850, with a wharf 180 feet long. John Howell's shipyard launched the last Penclawdd-built vessel to survive—the *William Henry,* in 1838. A schooner of 110 tons she made several voyages to the Mediterranean; sold to Holyhead she was still afloat in 1900.

Llanelli's first dock was built in 1836: forty years later the port was dispatching nearly 300,000 tons of coal annually from the North Dock, photographed here with the Montrose-built barquentine *Standard* in the foreground. The attractive foliage decoration at the stemhead of the *Standard* was frequently employed for vessels without a figurehead. A steam crane, itself now an object of historic interest, stands in the background, among the endless rows of coal-trucks.

10   Barquentine *Standard* at Llanelli

Carmarthenshire's little ports have now also been deserted, except by yachtsmen. Burry Port saw its last trading vessel in 1924; Pembrey's little harbour built in 1810 has long silted up, and the coming of the railway to Kidwelly made the port redundant more than a hundred years ago. Carmarthen's deserted quay and sand-choked river give little evidence of a seaborne trade which dated from Roman times. In 1831 51 vessels were owned here and 420 coasters visited the port. Shipbuilding was carried on at the Pothouse Bank to the west of the Island Wharf the largest vessel launched here being the barque *Princess Royal*, 330 tons, in 1841. She made only two voyages, from London to Calcutta, and Liverpool to Cuba, before being lost—a major disaster for the shareholders and local insurance company which probably hastened the demise of Carmarthen shipbuilding, although the iron and tinplate works on the banks of the Towy flourished until 1902.

The *Annie Christian*, renamed *Ade*, built as a two-masted schooner for the coasting trade by William Westacott of Barnstaple, and later re-rigged as a ketch after sinking in the Mersey, lies at Saundersfoot Pier, built in the 1830s, and once crammed with coal brigs exporting the local anthracite. The tall scaffolding which once marked the sites of the collieries, the tramroads leading to the harbour and the long wooden funnels alongside the wharves through which the ships were loaded, have all gone—the last cargo being shipped out in 1930. Large sailing vessels were once built here by Francis Beddoe whose shipyard lay on the seaward side of Railway Street (now the Strand).

11   Saundersfoot

The chaos in Tenby's little harbour on the North Sands after the great storm of October 8th 1896, when a southerly gale veering southwest, raged all day, piling up a very heavy sea, in the worst storm in living memory. Although primarily a seaside resort and fishing port much frequented by Brixham trawlers before 1914, the three good anchorages in the Tenby area—Caldy Road, Tenby Road and Man o' War Road attracted many sailing vessels running for shelter, but they could be death-traps in sudden changes of wind.

12   'After storm' 1896

From Pembroke the two arms of the River Cleddau, eastern and western, stretch so deep inland that no part of Pembrokeshire is more than seven miles from salt water. Sailing vessels once plied here with cargoes of all kinds. Blackpool Mill marks the highest point of navigation on the Eastern Cleddau and vessels of 80 tons tied up here and loaded with corn. Haverfordwest at the head of the Western Cleddau could be reached by vessels of up to 200 tons. The shipyards which once flourished in the shadow of the ruined Priory of the Austin Friars have vanished—the building of the railway in 1853 ended Haverfordwest's sea-trade, but a pub called the Bristol Trader and some fine warehouses are relics of a once active commercial life.

Milford Haven is a great natural harbour twenty miles long with ten miles of deep-water anchorage. In 1790 the town of Milford was built by Sir William Hamilton, the friend of Lord Nelson. This is an unusual photograph showing Milford in 1860 when Hubberston Pill was practically dry at low tide. On the right is Hakin and on the left Milford with its quays. In the distance is the wooden pier built by Colonel Greville, a local landowner and great-nephew and heir of Sir William. Colonel Greville had a lifelong interest in ships and according to his obituary in 1867 'sacrificed his fortune to promote the prosperity and develop the resources of this place'—a dream which eluded him, for all his pet projects: whaling, the Naval Dockyard, the Irish packet service, the trans-Atlantic trade, came to nothing. The foundation stone for the Docks he had planned in Hubberston Pill was laid in 1864 but little progress was made until after his death.

13   Milford Haven

The northcountryman T. L. Oswald, formerly of Oswald, Mordaunt & Company of Southampton, where he built both iron and steel ships, moved his shipyard to Milford in 1890 and built the full-rigged ships *Speke* (above) and *Ditton* in 1891, both for Leyland Brothers of Liverpool. In 1892 he launched the massive steel barques *Lyderhorn*, 2914 tons, and *Windermere*, 3050 tons, the former for C. E. de Wolf & Company of Liverpool and the latter for Fisher & Sprott. The *Windermere* became one of the famous Rickmer fleet and was renamed *Paul Rickmers*—she went missing in July 1902. The *Lyderhorn* was the last of de Wolf's well-known fleet of Cape Horners; she also was sold to Germany in 1910 and renamed *Jersbek*. After World War I she was taken over by the French Government and converted into a hulk.

14   The *Speke* of Milford Haven

The *Speke* and the *Ditton* were the largest full-rigged ships ever built by Oswald, but were too large for only three masts, so in spite of their lofty rig (crossing a mainskysail over a single topgallant sail) they were not renowned for their speed. But with their dry accommodation amidships they were popular with seamen.

The photograph below shows the *Ditton* in collision with the *Port Crawford* at Newcastle, New South Wales. After a voyage from South America the *Ditton* was being towed into the harbour in ballast by only one tug in squally weather. As she was passing the *Port Crawford* a fierce squall struck her, and the tug being unable to hold her, she struck the *Port Crawford,* bringing down her foremast; fortunately, although steel spars and rigging rained on the decks of the *Port Crawford* and the *Peebleshire* lying alongside her, there were no casualties except for an unfortunate sailor who was on the *Ditton*'s bowsprit when she struck. After a successful career as Britain's largest full-rigged ship she was sold to Norway in 1911 and renamed *Nordfarer,* subsequently her name was changed again to *Bragdo.* She was wrecked at Boobjerg in 1921.

15 'Collision'

The *Speke* went aground (right) on the night of 21
February 1904 in Kitty Miller's Bay, Australia, while
beating down the coast in ballast bound for
Melbourne, her captain having mistaken his course in
the dark, fortunately with the loss of only one life.

16 The *Speke* aground in Kitty Miller's Bay

Small ports crowd Pembrokeshire's indented coast: Solva with its landlocked harbour, tiny Porth Clais, Abereiddy, Porthgain, Abercastle and Newport, although it is now many years since the last ketches landed cargoes. The photograph taken at Porthgain in 1910 shows the tiny artificial harbour built between 1902 and 1904, crowded with ketches which carried away the produce of the quarries and brickworks. The graded hard-core produced here was the second hardest rock in Britain—millions of tons were exported to London to metal the streets; bricks were exported to Ireland. Business reached its peak between 1900 and 1914 but it never recovered after World War I and ceased altogether ten years later. On the left is the crushing and grading plant, and smoke pours from a steam crane on the quayside and the funnel of a motor coaster dwarfed by the tall masts, its sharp bow contrasting with the beamy ketches.

17   Porthgain Harbour in 1910

The Lower Town Fishguard, a quiet little village at the mouth of the River Gwaun with a tidal harbour protected by an old breakwater. In the 1700s there was a flourishing fishing industry here, catching pilchards which were salted and shipped to the Mediterranean. In 1792 fifty coasting vessels were based here varying from twenty to a hundred tons and trade with Bristol continued until the mid 1800s; corn was the chief export and the granaries can be seen beside the bridge on the right. The 40 ton sloop *Ranger* brought in cargoes of culm and limestone burnt in the kiln near the granaries, which was last used in 1880. The shipyards at Fishguard, along with those of Lawrenny and Newport built all the schooners registered locally before 1850, and cargoes of timber arrived here regularly from the Baltic and Canada. Its importance declined with the coming of the railway and the creation of the new harbour at Goodwick across the bay in 1908.

18   Lower Fishguard

Cardigan has been an active port since the Middle Ages, and massive stone quays and warehouses survive along the River Teifi, and were still in use until the last war when cargoes of sugar and coal were regularly delivered here. There are now plans to bring sea-trade back to the river, at present used only by pleasure craft. The photograph is taken from an engraving dated 1830: the two brigs on the right are discharging their cargo at what is now known as Spiller's wharf, their bowsprits are steeved up to occupy less room on the crowded river. On the left are three sloop-rigged fishing-boats or barges. The mediaeval bridge marks the lowest crossing-point on the Teifi and is still commanded by the remains of the Norman castle. Cardigan's trade in the 1800s was chiefly with Ireland exporting corn, fish and slates (from Cilgerran) and importing salt, timber and coal. Between 1790 and 1866, 142 ships were built here by David Owens, David Griffiths and John Williams, among others. Across the river at St. Dogmael's, George Bowen built smacks and schooners including the 34 ton smack *Alice,* lost during the *Royal Charter* gale in 1859, and the 44 ton schooner *Eugenie,* built in 1853 and run down in St. Bride's Bay in 1864.

Cardigan's customs house controlled all creeks and harbours from Fishguard to Aberaeron.

19   Cardigan

Although only a handful of houses along the narrow Hawen valley, Llangrannog was an active port from 1750 until World War I, with small locally-built ships of thirty to sixty tons carrying goods around the coast between Bristol and Liverpool; salt was also brought regularly from Ireland. As late as 1875 a shipyard stood on the north side of the beach. Not all the ships built here were small—the *Anne and Catherine* launched in 1870 was over 300 tons: because there was no slipway a channel was dug for the occasion from the sea to the yard and the vessel safely launched was then towed to New Quay to be rigged. The vessels in the photograph are the schooners *Marged Ann* and *Liza Jane.* The *Marged Ann,* the smaller of the two, was owned by Captain Parry, The Ship, Tresaith; the Ipswich-built schooner *Elizabeth* or *Liza Jane* as she was familiarly known was owned by Evan Jenkins, lime and culm merchant of the Pentre Arms, Llangrannog. She was the last Llangrannog ship to bring a cargo of coal from Swansea in 1912; since the tides were not high enough she had to be unloaded some distance from shore—a storm came and the vessel was battered against the rocks and became a total loss. The same fate also befell the smack *Albatross* built in 1847 at Milford and also owned by Evan Jenkins.

20 Llangrannog

Culm and coal were the most frequent imports in recent times, with the general cargo regularly brought to Llangrannog. The coal-dust fuel known as culm was in general use in Cardiganshire because of its cheapness as fuel when mixed with clay.

In discharging cargo at Llangrannog, it was essential to get the vessel sailing once again on the following flood tide, or disaster could follow as in the case of the *Liza Jane*. Three carts were used to each ship and were hired from local farmers at the rate of five shillings per tide. Five or six local labourers were hired to raise the culm in large buckets from the hold with the aid of a pulley fastened to a spar suspended from the vessel's mast, and a well-trained horse that paced to and fro. The culm was dumped on the deck and two more labourers shovelled it along a shute to the waiting cart.

Lime was an equally popular commodity because Cardiganshire soil is especially deficient in lime and every coastside village had at least one limekiln. One can be clearly seen on the right of the photograph of Aberporth in 1872, its small beach crowded with smacks unloading into a constant procession of carts.

21   Aberporth

A schooner unloads coal at New Quay's pier in the early 1900s. An air of somnolence lies over the quay, echoed in the seated line of old salts at Cnwc-y-Glap on the left, the traditional gathering place of the village worthies. New Quay was obviously no longer a busy port although sailing ships still occasionally brought in coal or culm, groceries and china, but in its heyday from 1830-70 twelve yards and six smithies were kept fully employed in turning out brigs, brigantines, schooners, smacks and barques of up to 300 tons. Fewer than a dozen of these survived beyond World War I. The majority were engaged in the coasting trade but a number sailed regularly to the Baltic, the Mediterranean and North and South America.

Above the quay stands the Blue Bell, one of the twenty-four inns which catered to the mariners and shipyard workers and behind it is the last and best known of the three Sailrooms, that of John Jones who supplied sails for nearly all the ships built along this coast, as far away as Swansea.

22 Unloading coal at New Quay

Mentioned in the Elizabethan Port Books, Aberaeron became a busy little harbour for trade in slate, limestone, grain, coal, timber and pigs, after the Rev. Thomas Alban Jones Gwynne obtained a Harbour Act in 1807 to repair and improve the existing ruinous quays. At least seventy-five vessels were built in the town the last being the *Cadwgan* launched in 1883 which may be among the seven ketches at anchor in this photograph of Pwll Cam the inner harbour.

23 The port of Aberaeron

The *Cadwgan* was built by David Jones, nephew of Evan Jones, shipbuilder of Llanddewi Aberarth: his yard there was destroyed by a violent rainstorm in 1846, during which the 74 ton schooner *Adroit* then under construction, was washed out to sea and subsequently towed into Aberaeron and completed there in the yards on the south beach. Thereafter Evan Jones worked at Aberaeron: he and his nephew producing sixteen schooners which were noted for their speed. The *Pleiades,* built by David Jones, in 1866, when outward bound for Spain, passed a four-masted barque returning to England: the *Pleiades* discharged her cargo and overtook the barque on the return voyage. Like the other Aberaeron shipwrights the Harris family, David Jones always worked from the half-model and that of the *Cadwgan* is one of the few to have survived. Below in Aberystwyth harbour is his tiller-steered schooner, the *Aeron Belle,* launched in 1856.

24 *Aeron Belle*—schooner believed built near Aberaeron

Aberystwyth is now better known as a holiday resort and university town, but from the middle of the 1500s to the end of the 1800s it was an active port initially engaged in the herring trade and exporting bark to Irish tanneries. But it was the development of the lead trade after 1700, with the opening up of the lead mines in north Cardiganshire, which led to Aberystwyth's greatest prosperity: from the 1750s thirty to forty ships were continually employed every year in carrying up to 4,000 tons of lead and zinc ore to other British ports, and these remained the chief items in Aberystwyth's sea-trade until this was gradually killed by the coming of the railway in 1864. This photograph of Aberystwyth in the 1880s shows several types of the vessels which frequented the port, on the left is a fore-and-aft rigged three-masted schooner and ahead of her a two-masted topsail schooner; on the right is the Iron Screw schooner *Henry E. Taylor* owned by the Aberystwyth and Cardigan Bay Steam Packet Company, and in front of her one of the many little sloops built at Aberystwyth in the shipyards at the Gap in the centre background from 1792 onwards.

25　Sail and steam vessels at Aberystwyth

The barque *Hope* of Aberystwyth, built by Labbie at Quebec in 1865, at anchor below the warehouses where the lead ore was stored. She was one of the innumerable Canadian built vessels which in the latter half of the 1800s competed with British built ships as it became more costly to import timber for shipbuilding. A vessel built in Quebec or Prince Edward Island cost 95 dollars a ton as opposed to 110 dollars a ton in Britain. Owned by John Evans of Aberystwyth, the *Hope* was lost off Cape Race in August 1892.

26   The barque *Hope* of Aberystwyth

This is the port of Aberdovey in 1890. On the left are two of the seven survivors of her once famous fleet of schooners. Aberdovey's prosperity like that of so many North Wales ports was founded on slate but her ships were to be found also in the exacting Newfoundland trade—a typical round voyage being slates to Cadiz, salt to St. John's, Newfoundland, ballast to Labrador and back to the Mediterranean with a cargo of salt fish. A large fleet of small sloops was also engaged in carrying a variety of cargoes up the Dovey, returning with lead ore from Derwenlas, but their employment ended in 1863 with the coming of the railway. Among the last vessels so engaged was the sloop *Milo* which was subsequently sunk, filled with stones, to act as a revetment at Llugwy where she had so often discharged her cargo. Aberdovey has become a seaside resort and at Derwenlas little remains also to remind one of its former activity— Quay Ward is commemorated by a name on a gateway and the tavern which once refreshed shipwrights and mariners is a private house; even the river has been diverted and where once ships sailed is now dry land.

27   Aberdovey about 1890: Fleet of Fishing Cutters
      in the background

The harbour at Barmouth before the railway bridge was built across the Mawddach, filled with schooners, ketches and smacks. In 1813 Barmouth owned a hundred vessels and was the main port for the woollen trade of mid-Wales, sending cloth to Spain, Portugal and South America. But the French wars struck a heavy blow at this trade and post-war recovery was disappointing; subsequently the bulk of Barmouth's trade was carried on with Bristol and ports between, Liverpool and Ireland. Several vessels were built here including the schooners *Ann & Elizabeth* and *Maria & Ellen* launched simultaneously in 1838. Barmouth was also the home port of the Newfoundland fleet of J. H. Lister. He owned four lovely schooners—the three-masted Western Ocean Yachts *Consul Kaestner, Jenny Jones* and *Royal Lister* built at Portmadoc in 1892, 1893 and 1902 respectively, and the Kingsbridge-built two-masted schooner *Cariad* credited with the fastest passage ever made from Newfoundland to Oporto, taking only ten days to cross the Atlantic. The *Consul Kaestner* was run down off Cape St. Vincent by the S.S. Jokai while on a voyage from the Isle of Man to Cadiz on 28 June 1902; the *Royal Lister* stranded on the coast of Morocco 27 February 1913 and became a total loss; and the *Cariad* and the *Jenny Jones* were sold to Newfoundland in 1916 and 1917. J. H. Lister was a keen amateur photographer and the first photograph of Portmadoc and that of Caernarvon are both his work.

28   The harbour at Barmouth

The ketch *Garlandstone* in Aberhamffra Harbour near Barmouth. The *Garlandstone*, launched in 1909 by James Goss at Bere Alston in Devon was one of the last wooden merchant sailing vessels to be built in Britain. In 1922 her topmast was sent down when she was fitted with a 40 h.p. engine. She remained a working vessel until the 1950s when she was converted into a houseboat. She lay at Aberhamffra harbour until the spring of 1973 when she was towed to Portmadoc to be restored as a Maritime Museum.

29   The *Garlandstone* at Aberhamffra

Portmadoc grew up in the 1820s alongside the massive embankment built to reclaim 2,000 acres of land at the mouth of the River Glaslyn, by William Alexander Madocks who laid out the town of Tremadoc there. Although the development of the port was a secondary consideration, by 1825 it was working excellently exporting slates from the quarries of Ffestiniog; in 1862, 114,000 tons of slates were being exported annually. But competition from the railways increased and by 1890, 50% of the slates were carried in this way. Portmadoc was still a busy port: the photograph below taken in 1889 shows the entrance to the harbour. On the left is the Caernarvon-owned schooner *Twelve Apostles* built at Pwllheli in 1858; she was driven ashore in a north-easterly gale on 23 November 1898—the announcement being made at Lloyds that the *Twelve Apostles* had vanished into Hell's Mouth on the Lleyn Peninsula, the notorious grave of a host of ships. Beyond her is the brig-rigged *Wild Rose*, launched as a brigantine in 1863 by Gardner at Sunderland and owned at Caernarvon.

30   The entrance to Portmadoc Harbour, 1889

The quays of the inner harbour at Portmadoc are
piled with slates. A ketch awaits her cargo and
schooners and brigantines are tied up along the
quays. The tracks along which the trucks travelled
with their loads can be seen here and there among the
stacks of slates.

31   Portmadoc Harbour

In the last days of sail, Portmadoc became famous the world over for its 'Western Ocean Yachts', the graceful powerful three-masted schooners built primarily for the Newfoundland trade, like the *Dorothy* above, launched by David Jones in 1891. These schooners were the equals in speed of anything carrying sail in the North Atlantic and the *Blodwen* made the record run from Indian Tickle, Labrador, to Patras, Greece in 22 days. Their rig made it possible for them to be handled by a smaller crew than brigs or barquentines, an important consideration when sail was competing economically against steam and freights were falling. But the Newfoundland trade was one of the last in which it was more profitable to employ sailing ships—steamers were not suitable for the small harbours like Longtickle, Labrador where they could not refuel and there might be delays in loading cargo, since they relied on a quick turnaround for their profits. So the lovely schooners built by David Jones the originator of the design, David Williams and Ebenezer Roberts, continued to sail profitably until World War I; the last, the *Gestiana* being launched in 1913 by David Williams, but she was lost on her maiden voyage between Newfoundland and Cape Breton Island—a crippling financial loss for Portmadoc shipbuilding.

32   The *Dorothy* at Portmadoc

33   The *Edwin*

Pwllheli was the main port of the Lleyn for centuries, a pier being built here in the reign of George III. In 1903 an inner harbour was provided but because of the continual silting of the river in the outer harbour which obstructed the approach it was seldom used except by a few timber ships. Below is the wooden schooner *Edwin,* one of the 460 vessels built here between 1759 and 1878. The *Edwin* launched here in 1873 by David Williams, is seen off the coast of Morocco a dangerous and harbourless shore where all trading was done off the beaches; it was the bane of ships calling here to load grain. She spent most of her life in the Newfoundland trade and was broken up in 1921. Ten vessels in all came from David Williams' yard including the last ship launched at Pwllheli— the schooner *W. D. Potts* launched in 1878. A clipper, the *W. D. Potts* carried slates from Portmadoc to the Elbe, a distance of a 1000 miles, in five days, averaging 200 miles a day; the slate trade was a hard one, the dead weight of the cargo placing a great strain on the vessel, but year after year Pwllheli schooners turned in equally good performances. The *W. D. Potts* was sunk by a submarine off the Wigtownshire coast in 1917.

The natural harbour of Porthdinllaen lies in the Southern part of Caernarvon Bay, providing a safe anchorage. In 1866 the Porthdinllaen Harbour Company began to build a breakwater and make wharves here, but the hope that it might replace Holyhead as the packet station for Ireland was not realized. Fifty-eight vessels were launched here in the 1800s, the last being the brigantine *Annie Lloyd* built by Hugh Hughes in 1878 and lost at the Bahamas in 1907. The largest vessel built here was the wooden barque *Robert Jones,* 495 tons, launched by James Owen in 1866 for Robert Rees of Morfa Nevin.

34 Porthdinllaen Harbour

The ketch *Zion Hill* built as a schooner at Nevin in 1866 by Evan Thomas is getting a touch of paint below Caernarvon Castle. She was sold to Wexford in 1891. A few yards to the right is the great Slate Quay from which thousands of tons were exported annually. Between 1758 and 1898, 225 vessels were built here by Samuel and Richard Samuel, Roberts and Company, William Jones, Thomas Williams and Richard Price among others.

Caernarvon was the home port of the 60 ton smack-rigged flat *Ann* built at Frodsham in 1799 and immortalized as *Fflat Huw Puw* in several Welsh sea shanties. Captain Huw Puw was born at Liverpool in 1795 but settled in Caernarvon. The *Ann* was wrecked on St. Tudwal's Island on 18 October 1858.

35   The *Zion Hill* at Caernarfon

A peaceful evening in the Menai Straits with schooners and a brigantine at anchor. The schooner on the left has the Irish sea stern with the rudder out of doors in sharp contrast to her immediate neighbour which is a graceful little vessel with a counter stern. In the background is Bangor with its harbour, the Garth, crowded with shipping. Sixty-four ships were built at Bangor: two of the most active yards were those of John Parry and Edward Ellis the former with eleven vessels to his credit and the latter with nine. One of the last Bangor-built vessels still afloat was Ellis's brigantine *Sarah Lloyd,* launched in 1855 she was abandoned at Runcorn in 1936.

36   The Menai Straits

Port Dinorwic is the 'Felinheli' referred to in *Fflat Huw Puw*. In 1824 the owners of the Llanberis Slate Quarries built a dock here, appropriately with massive slabs of slate. It still survives virtually unaltered, surrounded by ruined warehouses, a reminder of the vanished days of the slate boom which ended when the competition from the cheaply produced foreign tiles became too much for the native product. Below, four vessels are in the little harbour leading to the dry dock at Port Dinorwic, in the background on the left masts emerge from the older dock. The quay is stacked with slates but everyone appears to have stopped work for the photographer. The smack-rigged vessel on the centre has an exceptionally tall topmast dwarfing the four schooners around her. The schooner on the left has her lower yard cockbilled to allow her to come alongside. A ketch waits at the entrance of the harbour. In 1849 Rees Jones moved his shipyard from declining Barmouth to busy Port Dinorwic and built twenty-eight vessels here the last being the schooner *F. K. Muspratt*, 80 tons, owned in Liverpool. Twenty-one of the vessels he launched were schooners, but he also built brigs, a brigantine and three barques including the *Ordovic*, 825 tons, launched in 1877, the largest vessel ever built in North Wales, lost at Cape Horn in 1894. Rees Jones and his son William also had shares in the Gwynedd Shipping Company which owned the iron barques *Moel Eilian* and *Moel-y-Don* and the iron four-masted barque *Moel Tryfan*, all built by W. Doxford & Sons of Sunderland in the 1880s.

37   Port Dinorwic

Holyhead is Britain's third largest passenger port and has always owed its importance to its position in relation to Ireland which made it the chief port for Dublin, mail and passengers for Ireland having been carried from it for centuries, although not always in comfort: Dean Swift, a regular voyager, wrote bitterly:

> Lo here I sit at Holy head
> With muddy ale and mouldy bread;
> I'm fastened both by wind and tide
> I see the ships at anchor ride . . .
> The Captain swears the sea's too rough—
> (He has not passengers enough).
> And thus the Dean is forced to stay,
> Till others come to help the pay.

The Inner harbour was built for the packet trade in 1821 with two handsome stone buildings which still stand—the Customs House and the Harbour Office with a small square clock-tower. But in the period covered by this book steam had long ousted sail on the Irish run and Holyhead is of interest primarily as a harbour refuge, the only one (save Milford Haven) between the Clyde and Land's End, which ships could enter at low tide. Below in a photograph taken in 1901 thirty-nine schooners are drying their sails in the shelter of Holyhead's magnificent breakwater one and a half miles long and enclosing an area of 677 acres. Designed by J. M. Rendell who also constructed the docks at Birkenhead it was begun in 1855 when the inner harbour was becoming congested, and opened in 1873. As late as 1917, over a period of eleven weeks, more than 250 vessels were wind-bound there according to a member of the crew of the two-masted topsail schooner *John Gibson* of Fleetwood, which had been forced to run for shelter there, loaded with coal from Runcorn for Ballinacurra.

38   The breakwater at Holyhead

Amlwch harbour is a natural creek between high cliffs, which dries out at low tide. In the 1700s the present harbour was constructed to accommodate the numerous vessels carrying copper ore from the nearby mines at Parys Mountain to Swansea. But the poor quality of the ore and competition from the new mines in South America and Africa led to the gradual closure of Anglesey's mines. In the photograph the copper ore hoppers and warehouses on the right are already in ruins and so are many of the houses once occupied by the hobblers and porters. Three schooners are alongside the quays, approached rather precariously by a couple of planks and a ladder, and securely moored at bow and stern by ropes stretching the whole width of the tiny harbour. The vessel in the centre is the schooner *Alice & Eliza* built at Lancaster. The last vessel owned in the port of Amlwch was the *Kate* built at Peel, Isle of Man in 1872—she burned out in Moelfre Bay in 1933.

39   From a postcard view of Amlwch Port

Although Rhyl has long been a seaside resort, it was one of the last ports in North Wales to be visited regularly by sailing ships bringing in cargoes of timber from Scandinavia and Russia for the sawmills of Charles Jones & Sons at the Foryd and Rhyl. Above a brigantine discharges her cargo; alongside are two ketches and on the right a topsail schooner. On the right is the shipyard at the Foryd with the slipway for hauling a vessel ashore. On the left is a hulk and behind the sheds a topsail schooner lies at anchor.

40   The harbour at Rhyl

41   Shipyard at the Foryd

A party seems to be in progress aboard the heavily laden barquentine in the centre of the channel, on the left people queue for the ferry, and the lady with the parasol on the beach, the crew of the little Bermuda-rigged dinghy and the boy sculling his boat and his companion seem equally fascinated. On the right alongside the timber wharves a large fore-and-aft rigged schooner has discharged her cargo; the barquentine ahead of her is still unloading —a spar has been rigged with a gin block and the stacks of timber on the quay are growing.

From SHIP to RAIL.   RHYL HARBOUR.
Archangel Reds,   Floorings,   Bathurst Spruce,   Mobile Pitchpine & English Cement.
Vessels discharging at Messrs. Charles Jones and Sons, Ltd.,
Timber Importers & Sawmill Proprietors, Foryd & Rhyl.

Tele. Address
TIMBER, RHYL.   Established 1870.   Telephone
                                                                     No. 35.

42   Timber wharves at Rhyl

The Point of Air colliery, Ffynnongroew. The ketch is probably the *Tryfan* owned by Captain Isaac Williams, who carried coal from the Point of Air to Cardigan Bay ports and beaches, returning with farm produce to Liverpool. The output of the Point of Air collieries reached its peak in 1915 but by then most of the coal was carried in steam coasters.

The topsail schooner *Florence Petherick* of Whitehaven at Connah's Quay waiting to load Buckley bricks for Ireland. In the background is the entrance to the shipyard of Ferguson and Baird. Buckley bricks were also carried to Spain the return cargo being iron ore for Mostyn brought from Bilbao.

Connah's Quay near the point where the River Dee meets the sea, was one of the last ports in Britain to own sailing ships—its prosperity being founded on Buckley bricks, floor tiles from Ruabon and Staffordshire drainage pipes and the like: because of their fragility these cargoes required careful handling and stowing—steam requiring a quick turnaround in port and a fast sea passage irrespective of the weather was a non-starter in these trades.

43   Point of Air Colliery, Ffynnongroew

44 The *Florence Petherick* at Connah's Quay

The *Useful,* built in 1878, was one of the fine fleet of coasting schooners launched by the Ashburners of Barrow. When their fleet was dispersed in 1909 at Connah's Quay, the *Useful* was purchased by the Reneys who owned the largest fleet of sailing ships at Connah's Quay and were among the last British owners of purely sailing ships. In 1947 she was wrecked on the Isle of Man at Douglas Head. Sailing vessels were also owned by the well-known firm of coasting shipowners, Coppack Brothers, for whom the *Kathleen & May* (see page 80) was launched in 1900.

45   The coasting schooner *Useful*

Norwegian vessels like this brig brought cargoes of pit-props to Connah's Quay and then loaded pitch at Queensferry. Ahead of her is a two-masted schooner. In the background is the Queensferry Bridge known as the Victoria Jubilee Bridge, opened by Mr. Gladstone in June 1897. At Sandycroft, just across the Dee from Queensferry, William Patterson launched the *Royal Charter,* the most famous vessel built on the Chester River. This iron-built auxiliary steam-clipper, 2719 tons, was launched on 31 August 1855 from the Sandycroft Ironworks, fully-rigged with yards and sails at her topmasts. Her fate was terrible—returning from Australia she was battered to pieces on the coast of Anglesey on 26 October 1859 with the loss of 434 lives and more than £300,000 in gold bullion and other valuables.

46   Unloading pit-props near the Queensferry Bridge, Connah's Quay

Chapter 3
Shipbuilding

The four-masted barque *Mary* in Messrs. Mordey, Carney & Company's dry dock in Newport. The boom years of Newport's shipbuilding in the 1860s were long past when this photograph was taken: some of the leading builders were R. Griffiths & Son, Matthew and John Jones, the former Customs officer Richard Burton, Messrs. Pride & Williams and Wilmot & Hall, the peak years being 1866 and 1867 when 21 vessels were launched. But competition from the more cheaply built vessels of Quebec, New Brunswick and Prince Edward Island was fierce and between 1850-75 many of these softwood brigs and barques were owned in Newport. Most of these were relatively small vessels of 200-400 tons, the exception being one of the largest and finest vessels owned in Newport, the full-rigged ship *Norwood,* 1233 tons, built at Quebec in 1853 and purchased by William Childs Webb of Newport. But like many softwoods she had a comparatively short life foundering in mid-ocean in 1865 on a voyage from Quebec to Liverpool. The largest locally-built sailing vessel was the *Crawshay Bailey,* 682 tons, launched in 1866 by the Newport Dry Dock & Iron Shipbuilding & Shiprepairing Company. She was posted missing after leaving Batavia bound for San Francisco, on November 23rd 1869. In the 1880s with the transition from sail to steam proceeding rapidly shipbuilding gave way entirely to ship-repairing.

47   The four masted barque *Mary* of Newport

A very early photograph of a shipyard on the bank of the Tawe in Swansea, with Kilvey Hill in the background. The vessel being repaired is a two-masted fore-and-aft rigged schooner. The tide is out and a top-hatted man, perhaps the owner of the schooner, poses for the photographer, probably the Rev. Calvert Jones, to whose passion for photography we owe many fascinating pictures of Swansea in the 1840s. The seated man on the right is wearing a hat so like a helmet that he must be one of the many porters who frequented the harbour and were employed to unload cargoes. In 1855 porters discharging a cargo of Caernarvon slate from a schooner at Swansea received fifteen shillings and threepence all told; the trimmers loading coal for the return voyage were paid ten shillings and fourpence.

John Richardson who settled in Swansea in 1826 subsequently owned a large yard on the banks of the North Dock where he launched three large barques, *the Duke of Beaufort, Owen Glyndwr* and the *Marquis of Worcester,* designed for the Cuba and Chile trade. The Richardsons were shipowners as well as builders and at one time owned at least fifteen sailing vessels. One of the last Swansea-built vessels to survive was the 300 ton schooner *Pitho* launched in 1868 at the old Phoenix Dock by George Meager. She was still afloat in 1919.

48   An early shipyard at Swansea

This painting by Thomas Danby was made in 1860: it shows two vessels being built at Cei Bach (Little Quay) with New Quay in the background. As at New Quay they were built right on the beach being launched at the highest tides. The nearer of the two is probably the brig *Laura* launched in 1861 and the other is the smack *George Evans,* two of the twenty ships built here by Thomas James Thomas between 1847-65, including nine schooners, five brigs and two of the largest vessels built at New Quay, the barques *Prince Llewellyn* and the *Syren,* 300 tons, for the South American trade. The *Prince Llewellyn* foundered off St. Thomas in 1883 and the *Syren* was lost four years later, thirty-nine days out on a passage from Buenos Ayres to Britain. The last of his vessels to survive was the little dandy schooner *Thomas & Sons:* launched in 1860 she foundered in Carmarthen Bay in 1913.

49   Shipbuilding at Cei Bach, New Quay

The first vessel listed in the Customs Register as being built in Aberystwyth is the smack *Nancy,* 20 tons, built in 1768 which survived until 1852 when she was broken up. The last was the lovely schooner *Edith Eleanor* (page 79) built by William Jones in 1881. In the photograph below the brig *Sir Robert M'Clure,* 197 tons, has been hauled out at Aberystwyth harbour for a refit; felted and yellow-metalled she traded regularly between London and South America. Launched in 1866 the *Sir Robert M'Clure* was one of the last vessels built by the Evans family at Aberystwyth. Foulk Evans began work as a shipwright in the 1820s and was joined within a few years by his son John, the most prolific of Aberystwyth shipbuilders with nearly fifty vessels to his credit. Other Aberystwyth shipbuilders were Griffith Davies, Owen Jones, William and Richard Roberts, Louis Roderick, David Watkins, David Morris and David Thomas.

50   *Sir Robert M'Clure* on the stocks at Aberystwyth

Roger Lewis's shipyard at Aberdovey with his sloop the *Dovey Packet* and the brigantine *Anna Maria* in for repairs. The *Anna Maria* was launched as a brig at Dumfries in 1858, and the little *Dovey Packet,* 28 tons, was built in 1845, one of the seventy-nine vessels built in this little town between 1840-80. Roger Lewis was one of the three principal builders launching in addition nine schooners. He was something of an eccentric and the performance of his vessels reflected his idiosyncracies. His last vessel, the schooner *Sebrina,* foundered on her maiden voyage to Ireland in 1881.

John Jones built the largest number of ships at Aberdovey beginning with the *Jane Gwynne* launched in 1858 from his yard on the west side of Bryn Llestair or Picnic Island: iron bolts driven deep in the rocks are now the only indication of the activity that once flourished here between 1857-66 when John Jones laid down sixteen of the twenty-nine vessels he built. In 1867 the railway cut through this yard and that on the other side of the island, thereafter most of the ships were built at the other three yards at Penhelig. In some years John Jones employed all the available yards at Aberdovey and also upriver at Derwenlas and at Llugwy.

By far the ablest builder of the three was Thomas Richards who launched fourteen vessels at what is now a little park in the centre of Aberdovey. It is astonishing how little in the way of equipment was required to build these ships: when he died in 1880, his sheds, surplus timber and tools when put up for auction realised only £19/10/-.

51   Aberdovey

This photograph was taken in 1880 and shows shipbuilding and repairs being carried out on Nevin Beach where 125 vessels were built between 1760 and 1880. The vessel in the foreground on the slipway is the newly-completed schooner *Venus,* 120 tons, built by Griffith Owen, the last vessel to be launched at Nevin. She was wrecked off Lisbon in December 1900. The two vessels in the background being repaired are the schooners *Harriott* and *Slater.* The *Harriott* was a small schooner of 43 tons built at Killhys, Donegal, Ireland, in 1857. She was owned by W. Parry of Edeyrn and was employed chiefly in carrying coal from the Mersey and Point of Air to Porthdinllaen and Nevin. The *Slater,* 102 tons, was built at Sunderland in 1858 and owned by Robert Preston, a slate merchant of Sunderland. The two hulks on the beach being broken up are the schooner *Mersey Jane* built at Nova Scotia in 1833 and owned by William Roberts of Nevin, and the schooner *Ann Roberts,* 37 tons, built at Nevin in 1856.

52   Nevin Beach in 1880

53 Conway

Between 1758 and 1891, 128 vessels were built at Conway by Thomas Robert and John Roberts, Richard Thomas and John Jones, the largest being the brig *Palanquin*, 304 tons, launched in 1842 by John Jones. Robert Roberts built up river at Caerhun where schooners of up to 80 tons were launched between 1819-55.

In the photograph of Conway's last shipyard beneath the walls of the Norman Castle there is much of interest: a smack is being extensively repaired, her deck planking being almost entirely renewed. Beyond is Conway's quay built in 1835 to facilitate the export of copper ore and slates, although owing to the proximity of Port Dinorwic and Abercegin (Port Penrhyn) Conway was only a minor slate-exporting port. Pitprops for the quarries are stacked in the background and two patient horses wait for work. Wooden sailing vessels from the Baltic continued to visit Conway until World War II—anchoring there to unload cargoes of timber for the sawmills.

This engraving shows the well-known yard of William Thomas at Amlwch with the dry dock behind the topsail schooner and an almost completed vessel on the slipway. Today a path from the harbour will bring one to the ruins of these sheds and chimneys the dry dock with the twisted wreckage of its gate and the sea-battered stones of the slipway. Shipbuilding at Amlwch was begun by the Treweek family as early as 1826. William Thomas purchased the yard in 1863 and built many wooden schooners here in the 1870s-80s, but it is for his iron and steel vessels that he is best remembered as they were considered to be among the finest ever launched. His first metal ship was the iron three-masted schooner *Elizabeth Peers,* built in 1885 and abandoned at sea in 1893. Then followed the *Detlef Wagner*, an iron barquentine 229 tons, launched in 1891. In 1893, 1894 and 1898 he launched the iron three-masted standing-topgallant yard schooners *Cymric, Celtic* and *Gaelic. Celtic* was lost in 1910 but both *Cymric* and *Gaelic* survived until World War II to make the last deep-water passages by British trading schooners. *Cymric* then owned in Ireland was lost on a voyage to Lisbon but *Gaelic* was still working up to the 1950s. William Thomas's son continued to build ships until 1908 when he launched his last vessel the *Eilean,* a three-masted steel auxiliary schooner which also survived as a working vessel until after World War II. He had a subsidiary yard at Millom, Cumberland.

54   From a drawing of William Thomas's shipyard
     at Amlwch

The iron barquentine *Detlef Wagner* built by William
Thomas for N. N. Nielson of Denmark in 1891, shown
fully-rigged and ready to launch. She was sunk by a
submarine in 1917.

55   *Detlef Wagner,* built 1891, by Wm. Thomas &
Sons, Amlwch.

Below is a photograph of local shipbuilders at Connah's Quay. The man at the end of the front row on the right is W. Baird, the foreman of Ferguson & Baird—one of the best-known firms of wooden shipbuilders, with more than fifty vessels to their credit since their beginning at Flint in 1859. They moved to Connah's Quay in the 1860s when the lease of their yard at Flint expired. The last survivor of their craft was the graceful *Kathleen & May* (page 80). The firm closed down in 1916 and the site of their slipways is now occupied by a timberyard.

56   The Ferguson & Baird's shipwrights

Chapter 4
Rigs

Sailing vessels are usually described by their rigs: that is the positioning of their masts and sails. During the 1800s these rigs became standardised although many variations from the norms still existed. Two main types of rig are recognised—square-rigged and fore-and-aft. On the square-rigger the sails were set from yards on the foreside of the mast, and any vessel with at least one square-rigged mast could correctly be described as square-rigged. Fore-and-aft rig can be defined as a gaff and boom sail set abaft the mast and a fore-and-aft rigged vessel was one on which all the masts were so rigged.

One of the oldest rigs still in use, which attained the height of its popularity in the 1860s, the era of the famous clippers *Thermopylae* and *Cutty Sark,* was the full-rigged ship, square-rigged on her three and sometimes four or even five masts, she could set as many as thirty-five sails (on the three-master), up to forty-seven on a huge five master like the German *Preussen*.

Below is the Ditton, the iron full-rigged ship launched at Milford Haven in 1891 by T. L. Oswald (see page 29) a typical example of this type of vessel.

57   The *Ditton*

This is the steel four-masted barque *Crocodile,* 2555 tons, built at Southampton in 1892: square-rigged on three masts, the fore, main and mizzen, and fore-and-aft rigged on the last, called the jigger. In order to meet the demand for larger vessels to carry big cargoes all over the world, this rig was developed in the 1880s-90s. These powerful four-masted barques could carry several thousand tons of cargo and could compete successfully with steam in some long distance trades. So successful were they that new vessels of this type were launched as late as 1926 and commercial voyages continued to be made until World War II. The last of the great fleets being that of Captain Gustaf Erikson of Mariehamn in the Aland Islands.

The *Crocodile* was one of the four large sailing ships built by the Southampton Naval Works Ltd, the others being the steel full-rigged ships *Agnes,* 2199 tons, *Dalgonar,* 2665 tons, and the *Annie Maud,* 2036 tons, all launched in 1891-92.

A typical voyage for such a vessel was that made by the *Crocodile* in 1908, when owned by W. Thomas & Company she left Barry Dock loaded with coal for the West Coast of South America; safely past the Horn and having discharged her cargo, she sailed in ballast for Australia where she collected a cargo of coal in New South Wales for Valparaiso, whence she shipped a cargo of salt-petre for Germany, and so home after a voyage of twenty-two months. She was considered a fast sailor although she does not appear to have broken any records. In 1915 she was sold to Norway for £9,500.

58   The *Crocodile*

The barque *Pride of Wales,* 298 tons, shown here leaving Amsterdam for Java, was built at Portmadoc in 1869 by Simon Jones. For most of her arduous life at sea she carried slates outward bound from Portmadoc, returning with phosphates. She was the largest vessel yet launched in Portmadoc and no expense was spared by her proud owner Capt. David Morris to make her as her name implied, one of the finest vessels ever launched there. Perhaps because of this she survived two tornadoes in the Caribbean. Since her first voyage was destined to be in Indian waters a skilful local carver decorated her stern with a jungle scene and her figurehead was a life-size representation of David Morris's daughter Jenny, whose son Capt. Henry Hughes subsequently recorded the barque's adventures in his history of Portmadoc *Immortal Sails.* The *Pride of Wales* both in size and sailing qualities was truly representative of her times. The three-masted barque, known merely as a barque, square-rigged on the fore and mainmast and fore-and-aft rigged on the mizzen, was along with the brig a very popular sailing rig for the larger of the small wooden sailing vessels in the 1800s, for every trade. Although they could vary from 250—2,000 tons in size, the 300 tonner was the most popular on the Welsh coast and was usually the largest type of vessel built in the little ports.

59   The *Pride of Wales*

The beautiful barquentine *Nymph* of New Quay built by Evan Daniel of Cei Bach was originally rigged as a brigantine at her launch in 1872. The barquentine rig—square-rigged on the foremast and fore-and-aft rigged on the two or more other masts became popular in the second part of the 1800s, because it was more economical both in maintenance and manning; and a barquentine was generally faster than a schooner of equivalent size. It developed from the American three-masted schooner, the rig being made known in Britain by the many barquentines built in Prince Edward Island and subsequently sold to British owners. The *Nymph*'s conversion may have been influenced by the arrival in New Quay of the barquentine *Raymond* in 1876. Barquentines were frequently used in the Newfoundland trade. The *Nymph*'s career ended in December 1886 when she was abandoned at sea, her master and crew being landed at Bordeaux.

60   The *Nymph* of New Quay

The brig with its two square-rigged masts and a gaff and boomsail set from the main lower mast, was the most popular rig for the larger wooden trading vessels in the 1700s and the first half of the 1800s. This is the brig *Glanavon,* built by J. B. Jarrett at Nevin in 1862. 184 tons, she was 96′ long with a breadth of 23′ and a depth of 13′. After carrying slates to Europe for twenty-two years, she was lost off the River Weser in Germany in 1884.

61 The *Glanavon*

In typical nineteenth century fashion, the brigantine *Active* is square-rigged on the foremast only, a derivative from the brig rig: the change to fore-and-aft rig on the main, making a ship much lighter on gear and men and therefore more economical to run. The 97 ton *Active* was launched as a schooner in 1848 by Thomas Davies & Sons at New Quay, being built on the open beach at Traethgwyn, in a yard leased from John Evans of Morfa Gwyn for £2 a quarter. Here between 1821-55 when he went bankrupt, Thomas Davies built eleven ships. The *Active* was re-rigged as a brigantine in 1856. John Evans of Morfa Gwyn was her first master and he was succeeded by his son Francis Evans. The *Active* was condemned as unseaworthy in 1879.

62   Brigantine *Active*

This is the topsail schooner *Edith Eleanor,* 95 tons, off Naples, the last vessel built at Aberystwyth; launched by William Jones in 1881. The topsail schooner, a two or three-masted fore-and-aft rigged vessel with square sails set from yards on the fore-topmast was the most popular rig for smaller sailing vessels from 1850 onwards because it was economical to rig, crew and maintain. There were several variations on this rig: many like the *Edith Eleanor* had on the foremast, foreyard, lower topsail yard and upper topsail yard and were technically double topsail schooners. There were also standing topgallant-yard schooners with an extra yard above the eyes of the topmast rigging. Less common were those which set a single topsail and a standing or flying topgallant-yard sail above it.

63   *Edith Eleanor.* Built at Aberystwyth 1881

Here is the lovely *Kathleen & May* drying her sails at Weavers Basin, Swansea in 1955. Launched as a topsail schooner, the *Lizzie May,* by Ferguson & Baird at Connah's Quay in 1900, her yards were sent down when her auxiliary motor was installed. As she appears here, she is an example of a fore-and-aft rigged schooner, a rig more popular in the U.S.A. than Britain. The *Kathleen & May* continued to trade under the command of Captain Jewell of Appledore until 1960, the last British sailing vessel to do so. She is now preserved as a museum ship at Plymouth by the Maritime Trust.

The vessel in the foreground is the *Emily Barratt,* the last wooden sailing ship to be launched by the Duddon Ship-building Company in 1913. Like the *Kathleen & May* she was one of the last merchant schooners.

64 *Kathleen and May* drying her sails at Weavers Basin, Swansea, 1955

An unidentified ketch is drying her sails in Aberaeron's inner harbour, Pwll Cam, while the annual November fair is in progress on the quay. The ketch rig—with a tall mainmast and a smaller mizzen, both fore-and-aft rigged with gaff and boom-sails— developed in the 1800s. It was more economical to maintain than a schooner which accounts for its increasing popularity in the last days of sail and a number of schooners ended their careers as ketches. Ketches were used in the Newfoundland trade, but the majority, like this one, was engaged in coasting or fishing.

65   Aberaeron

Below is the smack *Eaglet,* 34 tons, of Aberystwyth, built in 1845 by John Evans, painted sailing past the Smalls lighthouse in Pembrokeshire. She was sold to Beaumaris in 1869. From 1700—1850 these single-masted vessels described as sloops or smacks, but more commonly as the former, were the most popular small coasting vessel often only seven or eight tons. All were fore-and-aft rigged but a few like the *Eaglet* set a square sail from the topmast. Smacks are known to have traded as far as the Mediterranean, and although temporarily superseded by brigs and schooners during the boom in shipping which began in the 1830s—in the last days of sail the few sailing vessels to be seen in any harbour are invariably smacks.

66   *Eaglet* of Aberystwyth

Chapter 5
Mariners and Mysteries

Below is the crew of the barque *Adventurer* of
Liverpool, seen on the right discharging ballast. In the
centre is the Captain, Edward Jones of New Quay,
and seated on the deck on his right is his nineteen year
old nephew Thomas Jones. The *Adventurer* was built
at Glasgow in 1875, and owned by Doward, Dickson
& Company of Liverpool.

67   Crew of Barque *Adventurer*

Edward Jones was born in a little cottage in the depths of the country several miles from New Quay in 1843; attracted by the boom in shipbuilding in New Quay, he went to sea as an apprentice earning seven shillings and sixpence a month, and gradually rose to command the larger vessels built there, including the barque *Syren*. When New Quay's prosperity declined, like many of her captains he turned elsewhere for employment, and was lost in the *Adventurer* with all hands, on a voyage from Taltal to Talchuano on the West Coast of South America, in March 1893.

68 Barque *Adventurer* of Liverpool

The career of Captain 'Dai' Williams

Captain David Williams was born to the sea, in the little Teify-side village of St. Dogmaels with a long history of shipbuilding. His father was lost off Cape Horn in the Swansea copper-ore barque *Georgina* in 1879 when David was three years old. After a brief spell as a pupil teacher because his mother was understandably reluctant to let him go to sea (although his school holidays were spent aboard locally owned schooners and barquentines sailing to the Mediterranean and Newfoundland which gave him valuable experience) he joined the barque *Cathaya,* trading to the River Plate, in 1893. By 1902 he had his master's certificate and then turned briefly to steam with the White Star Line. However when in 1910 the White Star Line bought the *Mersey,* a full-rigged ship, as a training vessel for their apprentices, Captain Williams returned to his first love as Chief Officer and was later appointed to the *Medway* a four-masted barque built as a cadet ship in 1902 by A. McMillan & Son. First owned in South America, she was acquired by Devitt and Moore in 1910. Under Captain Williams she sailed with her crew of apprentices in the Chilean nitrate trade throughout the First World War, earning good money while instructing the boys in the arts of seamanship in sailing vessels, then still required by most of the big steam companies for their officers. Although a fine sailing ship, capable of making 285 miles on her best day's run, by Government order the *Medway* was among the vessels selected in 1918 for conversion to an oil tanker and thus she ended her career. Captain Williams' career in sail ended with the *Bellands* (formerly the *Forteviot)*, a big four-masted barque of 3145 tons, built in 1891, which he took over in 1921, running her out to Australia and back to Falmouth

68a   *Medway*

with 5,600 tons of grain in less than eight months, her last voyage under the British flag for she was sold to Norway in 1922.

A genial and conscientious man, 'Dai' Williams' apprentices were the envy of all who served in the 'starvation ships' which many of the last British Cape Horners were, as the strict economy necessitated by declining freights forced almost unbearable conditions on their crews. He was one of the best of the last of the Cape Horn captains, 'a real sailor and a gentleman' as one of the *Bellands'* crew described him.

The master and crew of an unidentified barque, about 1890. The captain was David Davies of New Quay, who after a lifetime in sailing ships and twenty years in command would be earning at most £320 a year. An Able Seaman would earn £4 a month, and for that money in such a vessel he would face long hard voyages, probably including at least one rounding of the dreaded Cape Horn annually: there in winter he could expect to go for many days without hot food or dry clothes and such meals as he obtained might be virtually inedible, ancient salt beef and iron-hard pantiles or ships' biscuits; frostbite and torn-out finger-nails were minor ailments to be faced while shortening sail in screaming gales and the ever-present risk of being plunged to instant death either in the raging sea or on the deck.

69   Captain David Davies and crew

Below are the captain (another David Davies) and crew of a coasting schooner the *Mary B. Mitchell,* with some of the porters ready to unload her cargo, in the 1890s. This steel three-masted schooner was built by Paul Rodgers at Carrickfergus in 1892 and survived to carry essential cargoes from Liverpool during the worst of the blitz, in World War II.

70   Captain and crew aboard the *Mary B. Mitchell*

This photograph taken in the 1920s shows the five members of the crew of the sailing coaster *Elizabeth Drew*: from left to right Jack Johansson, the mate, the two A.B.'s—Albert, with the ship's cat and R. W. Cheley, the Cook, Paddy O.S. and E. Gordon the Master. The *Elizabeth Drew* was a double-topsail two-masted schooner built by Stribley at Padstow in 1871; formerly a Newfoundland trader for Sims brothers, in 1919 she was acquired by the Hook Trading Company which exported anthracite from their tiny port on the River Cleddau. She was stripped of her topsail yards and fitted with a 50 h.p. motor. In 1933 while on a voyage from Blyth to Padstow she was run down and sunk in thick fog by a German liner the *Mimi Horn* but her crew was saved.

At the time this photograph was taken she carried coal from Hook to Treport in France at £6 per ton freight and returned with shingle ballast which was used for road-making around the Hook property.

71   Crew of the *Elizabeth Drew*

Captain John Jones of Aberaeron

The *Kildonan* was a ship of 650 tons built in Glasgow in 1869 and owned by W. B. Jones of Swansea. She proved to be a lucky ship for her master, Captain John Jones. Born at Aberaeron in 1846 into a very poor family, John went to sea at the age of 14 after his father, a ship's carpenter, had been drowned when a rowing boat capsized during the launching of the *Glynaeron* which he was following out to sea as was the custom. John's first voyage was on the schooner *Elizabeth* of New Quay, as an apprentice earning 7/6 a month. He was treated badly by the captain and broke a leg by falling overboard at Liverpool. When he recovered, he joined the *Liza Brown* as an Ordinary Seaman earning 13/- a month. On this ship the crew was kept so short of provisions that they nearly starved. For a time John Jones abandoned the sea and prospected for gold in Australia, but when his efforts were unsuccessful he wisely became a sailor once more. By 1873 he was in command of the brigantine *Albert,* built in Prince Edward Island, and subsequently commanded the *Chester,* the *Isabella,* the *Kildonan,* the *Lancashire* and the *Aigburth.* In 1883 as master of the *Kildonan* he received a prize of £191 for assisting the crew of the *Inchcape Rock* off Cape Horn, her master and four hands having been lost overboard in the mountainous seas. Jones and two of his crew risked their lives to carry replacements of nautical instruments in a tiny boat to the *Inchcape Rock.*

By the end of his career, as master of the *Aigburth* a full-rigged ship built at Workington in 1882, 1798 tons, owned by R. W. Leyland of Liverpool, John Jones was earning £320 a year as he proudly recorded in his autobiography, remembering the bitter poverty of his early life. He died in 1911.

72   Cranogwen

Sarah Jane Rees

Many of the small seaports of Wales seem from a study of their churchyards, to have been populated almost entirely by Master Mariners, and one observes how many rose high in their chosen profession, captaining large vessels, even directing large shipping companies, yet often born on farms remote from their future calling—how did they learn their trade? One answer is by practical example at a tender age—it was not unusual for a boy to go to sea at the age of nine or ten years, but more than this long experience would be required as the Board of Trade Examinations for licensing Captains became more rigorous, and to meet these requirements local schools often included in their curriculum of the three R's, training in Trigonometry and the principles of Navigation. Some schools indeed specialized in this work, and perhaps one of the most unusual was that directed by Sarah Jane Rees at Llangrannog, Cardiganshire. Born in 1839, as a girl Miss Rees regularly went to sea in her father's sailing vessel when he was short-handed on coastal voyages, like a number of her contemporaries, but she was unique thereafter when she came to teach in the village school and helped prepare local sailors for their navigation exams having qualified herself for the Certificate of Master Mariner. In Wales she is better known as "Cranogwen", her bardic name, having won the Crown for poetry in the National Eisteddfod, and also as the founder and moving spirit of the Temperance Union of the Women of South Wales. In addition she was a preacher, lecturer and the founder and editor of a woman's journal in Welsh which ran for thirteen successful years. She died in 1916.

The *Harry* of Swansea

The story of the voyage of the *Harry* of Swansea reveals the incredible endurance of Britain's merchant ship seamen in the sailing ship era. On April 12th 1893 the three-masted fore-and-aft rigged schooner *Harry,* loaded with coal for Pernambuco, sailed from the South Dock, Swansea with a crew of thirteen, an unlucky number for some if not all the men. Built at Nova Scotia, she was commanded by Captain Thomas Evans of New Quay, Cardiganshire and both her First and Second Mates were New Quay men. On the outward voyage they made a fair passage lasting thirty-eight days. Captain Evans was a good seaman and navigator but he was a cracker-on of sail and a driver. He was a short thickset man, very determined and courageous and treated his men well; there was good food fore and aft but the crew had to work. On arrival at Pernambuco they discharged the coal into barges in the harbour and after cleaning out the holds, a filthy task, took in a full cargo of sugar; all the cargo had to be loaded and unloaded with a hand winch and this heavy labour in the sultry heat of Brazil was a terrible strain on the men. No shore leave could be permitted because of the unhealthy climate and many seamen among the other vessels tied up there died daily from the dreaded yellow fever, 'Yellow Jack' as the sailors called it. Three days before she was due to sail the *Harry*'s cook fell ill with

73 The *Harry* of Swansea

the fever and died in the hospital soon after being taken ashore. As the second mate wrote subsequently, 'this was the commencement of our misfortunes and bad luck which followed us till the voyage ended'. They were glad to weigh anchor for Delaware U.S.A. for orders.

Within 24 hours the Mate Thomas Thomas sickened with yellow fever and ran about the deck in his delirium. He died the following day; a few days later William Evans the A.B. also died from the fever and it was an apprehensive crew which sailed on for Delaware fearing that Yellow Jack would strike yet again—it was not unknown in Swansea for vessels to arrive with their crews so decimated by the fever that there were not enough hands to bring the ships into port.

They reached Delaware without further mishap, the sugar was unloaded and Captain Evans received orders to proceed to Charleston to load a cargo of turpentine. At 6 p.m. on the evening after their arrival a terrific hurricane blew up hurling the *Harry* against the wharf; with great difficulty the crew struggled ashore being almost overwhelmed by the gigantic waves breaking over the ship. They had abandoned all hope for her as owing to the blackness of the night and the torrential rain they could see nothing but heard a constant smashing and grinding of timber. In the morning they saw that the force of the hurricane had wrecked the jetty and raised the *Harry* on to the piles, but as the water went down she slipped off in an upright position. She proved to be holed in two places but was quickly repaired, and the loading of the turpentine proceeded—it was not a desirable cargo for nothing could prevent the fumes from penetrating every part of the ship. For the duration of the voyage a special cabin was built on deck abaft the mizzen mast to avoid the fumes which were unbearable below. It was now late in October, a bad time to cross the Atlantic and a rough passage was anticipated. On the tenth day out of Charleston, a hurricane struck the ship like a thunderbolt: heavy seas broke over the deck and swept away the boats and spare spars lashed on deck: as these went they tore away the ventilators and the plates on which they were set, leaving large holes through which the sea poured into the holds. The Captain tried to run before the gale but a mountainous sea pooped her and wrecked the wheel, carrying the helmsman the length of the ship where by a miracle he was brought up by the foremast; the *Harry* lost way instantly, she broached to in the trough of the sea broadside to the force of the hurricane which put her on her beam ends on her starboard side. As she lay in this position with her holds full of water she was nothing better than a drifting derelict. The decks began to open under the pressure of the waves and it was only the buoyancy of her cargo which prevented her from sinking.

The crew were unaware of this and expected the worst as they huddled in the deckhouse although its shattered windows gave little shelter. There was no abatement in the fury of the gale. 'The seas were terrific and the high-pitched shriek of the wind in the shrouds and rigging as it rose in the worst of the squalls was almost deafening'. The Captain confided to Acting Mate Phil Jones that he had little hope for

their survival unless they could be picked up by another ship. As they crouched there together, Thomas Evans remembered that it was November 11th, the day of New Quay Fair—far away in New Quay the streets would be lined with stalls and children, theirs among them, would be clamouring for cosin caws and other traditional treats. But the morale of all the crew remained high—even the three Ordinary Seamen, boys of sixteen 'kept their heads like old hands'. By wading up to their armpits they could salvage food from the store-room and found bully beef and some wet biscuits though these were so tainted with turpentine as to be inedible, but they could not reach the fresh-water tank for three days and proper sleep was impossible in the constant pounding of the ship. However on November 14th when it seemed to the frozen and exhausted men that they could hold out no longer, the gale yielded slightly and the indomitable Captain at once ordered them to set the standing jib, the foretopmast, staysail and forestay sails to try and right the ship. It was a

SOUTH DOCK, SWANSEA

74   South Dock, Swansea

long struggle but slowly she came upright and under headsails only, ran through the night. A number of the crew had been injured in the heavy seas but the pumps were manned continually even by the injured mate whose knee had been dislocated: unable to stand he rigged a bell rope and pulled on that while sitting on deck. By the night of the fifteenth the water in the hold had been mastered. Fortunately for the weary crew a dead calm succeeded the gale and they were at last able to have the rest they sorely needed. On the second day of the calm they bent their fair-weather or old sails as they had no others left. It was also a noteworthy day as they had their first hot food and drink for over a week. But apart from the bully beef most of the food was uneatable through contact with the turpentine and the mainwater tank had become tainted with turpentine: drinking this water brought on terrible sickness.

A strong westerly wind enabled them to make good progress and a heavy rainfall went far to solve the water problem. Between 1 a.m. and 2 a.m. on December 6th Phil Jones sighted the Ushant light. The Captain as well as the crew after all they had endured were possessed with the desire of getting home and finishing the dreadful voyage as speedily as possible. Cramming on all the canvas they could, the ship flew up the Channel. 'We were overtaking and passing steamers and square-rigged ships . . . the old sails held well and our luck seemed to have turned for I would not have believed they would have stood what we gave them that day'. At Margate Sand Buoy they were taken in tow by a tug, two days later the voyage ended officially at the Globe Stairs Buoy just below Tower Bridge and the crew scarcely believing in their miraculous survival dispersed to their homes and families, all bearing the scars of the terrible voyage.

Phil Jones spoke for them all when he wrote: 'I have been going to sea all my life since I was ten years old and have rounded the Horn in sailing ships several times but I have never experienced anything to equal the fury of the hurricane that put the *Harry* on her beam ends. She proved herself to be a well-fastened and stoutly-built ship otherwise she could never have endured the strain she suffered in the terrific seas the hurricane put over her'. He survived to a ripe old age, but the memories of the *Harry*'s nightmare voyage remained indelible to his dying day.

The sea eventually claimed Thomas Evans as master of the full-rigged ship *Carnedd Llywelyn* which vanished on Cape Horn in 1908. Thomas Evans was no stranger to Cape Horn, on an earlier voyage in the same vessel he had been accompanied by his wife and daughter; but on this occasion the icefields drifting up from Antartica were more extensive than usual and it must be conjectured that the *Carnedd Llywelyn* struck a gigantic berg at night and sank. She was only one of a dozen large vessels which were simultaneously lost to the Horn.

As much discomfort and danger could be suffered on a coasting voyage as in deepwater as is shown in the following account by fifteen year old Roderick Cheley, of a voyage he made in 1917 as the Cook on board the two-masted topsail schooner *John Gibson* of Fleetwood, 82 tons, with three other crew, the Master William Davies, a Gloucester man, the Mate, also William Davies, his son, and an Irish A. B. Michael Fenton. Throughout the first World War innumerable small sailing vessels carried essential cargoes around our coasts braving the constant threat from submarines. Six Chester River vessels were lost in a single attack on a convoy off Falmouth in this same year and there was no War Risk Insurance for small coasting vessels so many little companies which suffered heavy losses in these years were never able to

Carnedd Llewelyn

replace their ships and in this way the war contributed heavily towards the decline in the numbers of sailing ships in Britain.

The *John Gibson* loaded coal at Runcorn for Ballinacurra, and towed down the Canal to Eastham Locks. Then with the wind light North-Westerly they slowly beat their way down the Mersey until they reached Rock Ferry where they anchored for a few days, having to keep an anchor watch because of the strong tides—the helm had to be shifted every time they swung. Having got a slant of wind they sailed down to Anglesey as far as Bardsey Island when the wind backed to the South West, dead ahead, and it blew hard and they had no choice but to run back to Holyhead. They were windbound in that harbour for eleven weeks along with two hundred and fifty other sailing vessels. During that time three vessels were blown ashore in the harbour, one being the two-masted topsail schooner "K.T." She lost her foremast, main topmast and bowsprit and was badly holed. She was later patched up and towed to the Mersey for repairs, then converted to a coal hulk. There were also several collisions caused by vessels dragging their anchors.

Young Cheley makes the point that no-one got paid overtime in these ships and however long the voyage took the money was that agreed upon when he first signed on. During the time he was in Holyhead the most money he received from the Old Man was sixpence per week, supposedly to buy soap and stamps as he was a stickler that Cheley should write home every week while in port.

> 'We went ashore about twice a week to report to the Agents, buy fresh bread and possibly get a paper for the Old Man. On occasions we did not lower the boat for over a week because of the wind and heavy seas. Some vessels lost their boats through keeping them afloat, because they broke adrift'.

When they eventually got away, they had to put into St. Tudwals's Bay to refill the water tank, and then four days later fetched Queenstown Harbour just about dark. They were challenged by a patrol boat which put a searchlight on them, whereupon the crew showed their name which was painted white on a black board, actually one of the skylight cover boards. 'They evidently could not read English as the patrol boat sent away an eight-oared boat in command of a Midshipman, who on getting alongside ordered us to "stop and go astern". The Old Man asked him if he knew what he was talking about as our topsails were already aback. The 'Middy' who was about my own age called, "Stop or I will board you". The Old Man replied, "Sonny if you come aboard I'll tan your backside, now go back aboard your ship and get someone to wipe your nose". He then yelled, "Alright Will, round yards and let her fill", and we bore away for Passage West where we anchored for the night'.

The following day a boat came down river from Ballinacurra with the Pilot and four hobblers: they hove anchor and partly sailed and partly kedged their way up river. The kedge was a hundred pound fisherman's anchor. The hobblers would take it in their boat with about sixty fathoms of light grass warp, leaving one end fast aboard the vessel. When they had rowed ahead to the limit of the rope they would drop the kedge and the crew would heave in the warp on their hand winch—this process was repeated as often as required.

The *John Gibson* tied up to the quay that evening, taking the ground every low water and the cargo was discharged the following day by the hobblers using the hand winch and 2 cwt. baskets. Every bit of coal was weighed on the quay with old fashioned scoop and weight scales, then the coal was hauled away by horse and cart. It took five or six days to discharge the full cargo of 160 tons. Then the crew had to scrub out the hold ready for loading oats in bulk. In the meantime the Irish A.B. who lived about seven miles away, returned home leaving only the mate and the boy to do all the work of the ship. After the hold had dried out and the limber boards were tight the hobblers began loading oats destined for Poole. The oats were carried on board in big sacks and emptied into the hold where the crew stowed it with large wooden shovels. It had to be packed tight in every corner, right up to the deckhead. When moving in the stuff they sank knee-deep and by the time the work was finished they were suffering severely from hay-fever. It took about 70 tons to fill the vessel and that was ten tons over her ballast trim.

They left Queenstown with a southerly wind and when two days out, the Old Man who always suffered from asthma became seriously ill and was confined to his bunk. The same night the wind backed to South East and started to pipe up; they shortened sail but the vessel was like an empty drum on the water and they were flung about in every direction. By dawn they had to reef her again and in stowing the boom jib Cheley slipped into the water but there was no time to change into dry gear. A heavy sea came aboard and smashed the sliding doors on the galley, and then another cleared everything moveable, pots, pans, stove lids, the lot, breaking the stove in the process. Now all they had left was the Old Man's small iron kettle and there was about 5 cwt of coal in the after peak under the cabin floor so they were able to keep the cabin bogey going. They ran out of bread and had to fall back on the hard ships biscuit about six inches square and an inch thick but there was margarine and corned beef as well as tea though with no milk and very little sugar.

The ship fortunately did not make any water. The mate and boy stood two hour watches as they drove out into the Atlantic, Cheley sleeping on the Cabin floor, and the mate when he slept at all, on the skylight top. Fifteen days out of Queenstown they sighted a light. The mate sent the boy aloft to count and time the flashes. He reckoned it must be St. Mary's on the Scillies, as indeed it was and within two days they were in Falmouth. The exhausted crew were assisted by fellow seamen from neighbouring vessels who escorted the Old Man to hospital and stowed ship while the mate and Cheley caught up on their sleep. The Captain turned out to have pneumonia and was in bed for two months, and Cheley, who was suffering from painful cuts and boils caused by the endless buffeting and the salt water, had to receive medical treatment. From the day the Captain had been taken ill, neither he nor the mate

had had time to wash, 'you can imagine what we looked—and smelled—like. I had to renew nearly all my kit in Falmouth which left me broke.'

After laying in Falmouth for a month they took the vessel to Poole to discharge the cargo. In spite of the amount of water they had shipped the cargo was practically undamaged. 'When we got paid I received two weeks extra pay which amounted to the princely sum of two pounds ten shillings.'

The Brig *Resolven*: **New Quay's** *Marie-Céleste*

New Quay has its own version of the *Marie-Céleste* story, its counterpart being the *Resolven,* a brig of 143 tons, built in Prince Edward Island in 1872 and owned in New Quay in 1873. New Quay shareholders owned a number of Canadian-built vessels, purchased through William Richards of Swansea, the Welsh agent for the Canadian shipbuilding companies, which because of the timber readily available to their yards were able to build such vessels more economically than in Britain and they were therefore cheaper to buy. Appropriately they were generally employed in the Newfoundland trade.

Captain J. Jones of New Quay was the master of the *Resolven* in the summer of 1885, when she carried a cargo of 143 tons of salt from Cadiz to Harbour Grace, Newfoundland. On August 27th, having discharged the cargo, the *Resolven* sailed for Snug Harbour, Labrador, to load salt cod destined for the Mediterranean. As was not unusual in those waters he took on three passengers for Snug Harbour. Sailing out of Harbour Grace passing the racks of drying fish and the fishing boats discharging their rich cargo from the Newfoundland Banks, there was no indication that danger lay ahead. But two days later, on August 29th, the *Resolven* was discovered derelict by the *Mülland* at the mouth of Trinity Bay, completely deserted, with her sails still set and a fire alight in the galley. The only indication of trouble was that her yard arms were broken and the running tackle dangled from the yards: the boat too was missing. The *Mulland*'s captain had observed a large iceberg in the area and it was assumed that the *Resolven* must have struck the iceberg in the night of August 28/29, the inexperienced master had decided to abandon his ship and the boat might have been swamped as it was pulling away from the ship by the sudden movement of the berg as the *Resolven* broke free of it; no trace of the crew was ever found. She was an unlucky ship and after a chapter of accidents, was lost at Newport, Nova Scotia, July 27, 1888.

The *Usk* of Newport

The strange story of the premonition of Captain Henry Mathias of the *Usk* ranks with that of the *Resolven* in Welsh sailing annals. The *Usk*, 368 tons, was built for Thomas Beynon and Co. of Cardiff at Newport in 1859. Her master Captain Mathias, a deeply religious man who, no matter how long his vessel might have been windbound, would not set sail on a Sunday be the wind never so favourable, took her in March 1860 out of Newport with a cargo of coal for Valparaiso. The voyage was uneventful until they reached the Falkland Islands, when the captain suddenly appeared on deck in the middle watch and ordered the crew to turn the ship for home, explaining in all seriousness that he had had a vision of God and received the message that if the ship did not at once return to Newport she would be totally destroyed by fire. Understandably he did not wish to risk the dangerous passage of the Horn with such a threat hanging over him. The crew were bewildered but obedient since the Captain seemed sane enough, giving orders as usual; but the rage of the owners when the *Usk* arrived safely back at Newport was equally understandable and Captain Mathias was instantly dismissed. He retired to his Pembrokeshire home having decided that the vision was a warning to give up the sea.

The coal was discharged at the Old Dock in case it might have become heated during the voyage and lay in the open for 14 days when it was reloaded and started once more on its long journey to Valparaiso, but when she had reached Calderon, off the coast of South America, after passing the Horn the coal began heating and although the *Usk* made Valparaiso Bay, as soon as the hatches were removed to fight the fire, she exploded into flames and was quickly destroyed. So Captain Mathias had the last laugh.

The wreck of the *Loch Shiel*

On the night of January 30th 1894 the iron full-rigged ship *Loch Shiel*, bound from Adelaide and Melbourne with a general cargo for her home port of Glasgow was caught in a severe gale off the Pembrokeshire coast and driven ashore on Thorn Island at the mouth of Milford Haven. Badly holed she began to fill rapidly, sinking at the stern. Hoping to attract attention from the shore a mattress was soaked in paraffin and burned. This distress signal was fortunately seen by the coastguard at St. Anne's Head who alerted the lifeboat at Angle. Meanwhile finding the ship firmly held by the bow the majority of the crew and the few passengers including a lady, succeeded in scrambling over the jib-boom and landing on the island. When the lifeboat, the *Henry Martin Harvey* arrived only six survivors remained on board, including an invalid passenger, and all were safely rescued by manoeuvring the lifeboat skilfully over the almost submerged wreck. Three of the lifeboat crew were then landed with ropes to haul up the remaining survivors from the inaccessible cliffs on which they had taken refuge, and eventually all, though weak and exhausted from exposure, were safely brought to the mainland.

There are many stories of heroism at sea and selfless endeavour by seamen to assist others of their kind in danger. Fortunately such stories as that of the loss of the *Priscilla* are rare. She was a small two masted schooner of 56 tons, built by John Evans at Aberystwyth in 1842 and was owned by her Master Thomas Parry and some of his relatives. On 22nd June 1845 the *Susannah* of Whitehaven bound from her home port for Newport, Monmouthshire, when passing Caldy Island between seven and eight o'clock observed a schooner capsized about three miles away. The *Susannah* went immediately to her assistance, sailing as close as she dared and her crew flung out fenders attached to ropes to the crew who were clinging to the hull, among them the master's wife and young child. But the vessel sank almost immediately taking down with her everyone still on board, the only survivor being a lad who had leapt off the capsized vessel as soon as the *Susannah* approached. William Stephen the sole survivor informed Captain Wood of the *Susannah* that the schooner was the *Priscilla* bound from Brockles in Donegal Bay for Gloucester with a cargo of oats. The wind was very strong and squally at the time and it was believed the cargo must have shifted. Stephens added that almost immediately after the *Priscilla* capsized he had seen a brigantine pass close by them

but without offering assistance. Captain Wood had also seen her and in his official report of the incident declared that if she had offered assistance all the crew might have been saved since she was not a third of the distance from the wreck that the *Susannah* was.

The wreck of the *Venus*

The 41 ton sloop *Venus* was built at Aberystwyth in 1805 and owned in Borth, trading along the Welsh coast. On June 6th 1857 she was on a voyage from Caernarvon to Aberdovey with a cargo of limestones. About 5 bells, it was blowing a strong gale from the west and the peak ties chain parted rendering the vessel unmanageable in the subsequent account of

76   *Loch Shiel*

her master Thomas Davies. Although so close to Aberdovey with only an hour's flood to run of the tide he dared not attempt to cross the treacherous bar, and being on a lee shore, 'I had no alternative but to run for the nearest beach which was effected about a mile to the southward of Aberdovey bar, seeing the vessel breaking up fast, I took to the sea, leaving the remaining three on board who all perished as the vessel soon went to pieces. After great exertion I landed in a very exhausted state'. So runs the report carefully filed in the Registers of Shipping deposited in the Customs & Excise Office in Aberystwyth. Those few brief paragraphs convey very clearly how narrow was the margin for error at sea, and the *Venus* was only one of many vessels lost within sight of port and safety.

The wreck of the *Bronwen*

There was no photographer around to record the fate of the *Venus,* but the death-throes of the schooner *Bronwen* of London were witnessed by a large audience, luckily for her crew. In September 1891, driven on to a lee shore by a strong westerly gale, like the *Venus*, she was fortunate to strike the coast at New Quay, just below the sheer cliffs of the Quarry Head. Here held fast in the rocks but steadily being pounded to pieces by the relentless waves she remained intact long enough for all her crew including the master's wife to be brought ashore by breeches buoy, cheered on by a huge crowd. The *Bronwen*'s nameboard is still preserved in the local Council's offices and below is one of several photographs of the wreck still in existence.

77 Wreck of the *Bronwen*

Books for further reading

Commerce & Customs (A History of the ports of Newport and Caerleon), James W. Dawson, 1932.

Cardiff: History of the Port, Edgar L. Chappell, 1939.

The Story of Swansea, N. L. Thomas, 1969.

The Story of Saundersfoot, T. G. Stickings, 1970.

The Story of Milford, J. F. Rees, 1954.

Pembrokeshire Sea-trading before 1900, Barbara J. George, *Field Studies,* 1964.

Ceredigion, the Cardiganshire Antiquarian Society's journal has studies of *Llangrannog,* 1964 and *Aberaeron,* 1969.

Brief Glory, D. W. Morgan, 1948, tells the story of Aberdovey.

Immortal Sails, Henry Hughes, 1969, relates the history of Portmadoc.

Holyhead, the Story of a Port, D. Lloyd Hughes & Dorothy M. Williams, 1967.

A Lifetime With Ships, Tom Coppack of Connah's Quay, 1973.

The Merchant Schooners, Basil Greenhill, 1968, has a chapter on the Irish Sea.

The Last of the Windjammers, Basil Lubbock, 1970, provides interesting accounts of the many large sailing vessels built on this coast.

Sailing Ship Rigs & Rigging, Harold A. Underhill, 1969, is the authoritative work on this subject.

Index

Reference to illustrations are printed in italic.